THE EVERYDAY POET

Poems to Live By

The Emergency Poet was conceived by poet and writer Deborah Alma as a fun way of bringing poetry to people.

A mix of the serious, the therapeutic and the theatrical, the Emergency Poet offers consultations inside her vintage ambulance and prescribes poems as cures.

Dressed in white coat and stethoscope, and accompanied by Nurse Verse or a Poemedic, she travels to literary and music festivals, libraries, schools, pubs, weddings and conferences.

Deborah works using poetry to help communicate with people with dementia and at the end of their lives, and taught the Writing Poetry module at the University of Worcester.

She has a BA in Creative Writing from the University of Birmingham and an MA in Creative Writing from Keele University, where she is currently Honorary Research Fellow.

THE
EVERYDAY
POET

Poems to Live By

EDITED BY

Deborah Alma
THE EMERGENCY POET

Michael O'Mara Books Limited

First published in Great Britain in 2016 by
Michael O'Mara Books Limited
9 Lion Yard
Tremadoc Road
London SW4 7NQ

A CIP catalogue record for this book is available from
the British Library.

Papers used by Michael O'Mara Books Limited are natural,
recyclable products made from wood grown in sustainable forests.
The manufacturing processes conform to the environmental
regulations of the country of origin.

ISBN: 978-1-78243-657-7 in hardback print format

1 3 5 7 9 10 8 6 4 2

Designed and typeset by Mark Bracey

Printed and bound by CPI Group (UK) Ltd, Croydon, CR0 4YY

www.mombooks.com

CONTENTS

Introduction   9

Try to praise the mutilated world   11
O taste and see   39
The washing never gets done   56
Let me count the ways   78
It feels like going home   114
Field guide   146
The spaces where breath goes   161

Acknowledgements   174
Recommended reading   175
Credits   176
Index of poets   183
Index of titles, first lines and notable lines 185

In memory of my beautiful grandmother,
Jess Alma (1911–99). She loved poetry.

INTRODUCTION

I speak to people about poetry all the time. I travel all over the UK and have even travelled as far as New Zealand to prescribe poetry from the back of my vintage ambulance. My travels have taught me that most people don't regularly read poetry; even people who are book lovers – people who cannot imagine not having a pile of books by the bed with the anticipation of reading – even they are unlikely to have a poetry book in that pile.

That is why I do what I do; why I drive an ambulance and invite people to come in and talk about themselves and their reading habits: so that, as a poetry evangelist, I can help them find a place for poetry in their own lives.

This anthology is a collection of poems that are very familiar to me; that I love, and that I would like to recommend as accessible poems that encapsulate the everyday, and it is especially for those who do not regularly read poetry. They are poems that start small – many of them emerge out of the detail of life's mundanities; they are of a world that we might recognize, about what it is to be human, to live and love and to get up in the morning.

As the Emergency Poet, I have also learnt that it's quite difficult to develop a habit of reading poetry: we are so easily distracted by our own busy lives. We may make time to read a novel in bed at night, but few of us seem to find a place for poetry. I often speak to people about how important it is just to leave poetry lying around the house, so that in a quiet moment, with a cup of tea, we might pick it up and be refreshed, challenged or stimulated. I recommend this anthology as perfect to leave in the bathroom, on a coffee table, in a waiting room or in the kitchen by the kettle.

TRY TO PRAISE THE MUTILATED WORLD

So often these days we shake our heads at
a world that can seem crazy and terrible,
which we struggle to make any sense of.
Poetry is at its best when it can help to
make a little sense of what it is to be alive
and gives us some of the meaning we search
for. The poems in this chapter are hopeful,
even against the odds.

Try to praise the mutilated world

ADAM ZAGAJEWSKI

Translated By Clare Cavanagh

Try to praise the mutilated world.
Remember June's long days,
and wild strawberries, drops of rosé wine.
The nettles that methodically overgrow
the abandoned homesteads of exiles.
You must praise the mutilated world.
You watched the stylish yachts and ships;
one of them had a long trip ahead of it,
while salty oblivion awaited others.
You've seen the refugees going nowhere,
you've heard the executioners sing joyfully.
You should praise the mutilated world.
Remember the moments when we were together
in a white room and the curtain fluttered.
Return in thought to the concert where music flared.
You gathered acorns in the park in autumn
and leaves eddied over the earth's scars.
Praise the mutilated world
and the gray feather a thrush lost,

and the gentle light that strays and vanishes
and returns.

Lowedges

HELEN MORT

And if those doors to other worlds exist
you'll find them here: Lowedges, where the city
smooths its skirt down in the name of modesty,
picks up its jacket, calls it a night. Here, bichon frises
chase their tails all morning on the astroturf,

a biker lets go of his handlebars and doesn't fall,
a woman rolls the afternoon into a cigarette
and smokes it silently. Forget the Cornish sea,
the top of Nevis with its trapdoor light…
If you're to leave this world, you'll leave it here:
this salvaged Friday, shop lights dimmed. Look up –
how easily the rain bisects the sky.

Quarantine

EAVAN BOLAND

In the worst hour of the worst season
　　of the worst year of a whole people
a man set out from the workhouse with his wife.
He was walking – they were both walking – north.

She was sick with famine fever and could not keep up.
　　He lifted her and put her on his back.
He walked like that west and north.
Until at nightfall under freezing stars they arrived.

In the morning they were both found dead.
　　Of cold. Of hunger. Of the toxins of a whole history.
But her feet were held against his breastbone.
The last heat of his flesh was his last gift to her.

Let no love poem ever come to this threshold.
　　There is no place here for the inexact
praise of the easy graces and sensuality of the body.
There is only time for this merciless inventory:

Their death together in the winter of 1847.

Also what they suffered. How they lived.
And what there is between a man and a woman.
And in which darkness it can best be proved.

Inefficient View of a Happy Man

ROBERT HARPER

I only saw him briefly,
as the train sliced off
a second of his life

to put beneath a pain of glass.
He carried branches
in his arms. On his face

a look beyond
contentment kept him
from sinking in the grass.

Composed Upon Westminster Bridge, September 3, 1802

WILLIAM WORDSWORTH

Earth has not anything to show more fair:
Dull would he be of soul who could pass by
A sight so touching in its majesty:
This City now doth, like a garment, wear
The beauty of the morning; silent, bare,
Ships, towers, domes, theatres, and temples lie
Open unto the fields, and to the sky;
All bright and glittering in the smokeless air.
Never did sun more beautifully steep
In his first splendour, valley, rock, or hill;
Ne'er saw I, never felt, a calm so deep!
The river glideth at his own sweet will:
Dear God! the very houses seem asleep;
And all that mighty heart is lying still!

Work without Hope

SAMUEL TAYLOR COLERIDGE

All Nature seems at work. Slugs leave their lair –
The bees are stirring – birds are on the wing –
And Winter slumbering in the open air,
Wears on his smiling face a dream of Spring!
And I the while, the sole unbusy thing,
Nor honey make, nor pair, nor build, nor sing.

Yet well I ken the banks where amaranths blow,
Have traced the fount whence streams of nectar flow.
Bloom, O ye amaranths! bloom for whom ye may,
For me ye bloom not! Glide, rich streams, away!
With lips unbrightened, wreathless brow, I stroll:
And would you learn the spells that drowse my soul?
Work without Hope draws nectar in a sieve,
And Hope without an object cannot live.

Today's Headlines

MEG COX

I was sitting next to the wood burner,
keeping warm, thinking about things,
like the snow, the spring, the news
and 300 circus fleas dead of cold.
They were doing OK, a regular job,
regular food, learning a trade.
Then they died of neglect.
None of us deserve that,
to be unfound at the stairs' foot,
dumped in a ditch, forgotten in a
cold house or trapped in a
box left outside in the cold
when you are only doing your best
in the one chance you have of life.

There will come soft rains

SARA TEASDALE

There will come soft rains and the smell of the ground,
And swallows circling with their shimmering sound;

And frogs in the pools singing at night,
And wild plum trees in tremulous white;

Robins will wear their feathery fire,
Whistling their whims on a low fence-wire;

And not one will know of the war, not one
Will care at last when it is done.

Not one would mind, neither bird nor tree,
If mankind perished utterly;

And Spring herself, when she woke at dawn
Would scarcely know that we were gone.

The Darkling Thrush

THOMAS HARDY

I leant upon a coppice gate
　　When Frost was spectre-grey,
And Winter's dregs made desolate
　　The weakening eye of day.
The tangled bine-stems scored the sky
　　Like strings of broken lyres,
And all mankind that haunted nigh
　　Had sought their household fires.

The land's sharp features seemed to be
　　The Century's corpse outleant,
His crypt the cloudy canopy,
　　The wind his death-lament.
The ancient pulse of germ and birth
　　Was shrunken hard and dry,
And every spirit upon earth
　　Seemed fervourless as I.

At once a voice arose among
　　The bleak twigs overhead
In a full-hearted evensong

Of joy illimited;
An aged thrush, frail, gaunt, and small,
    In blast-beruffled plume,
Had chosen thus to fling his soul
    Upon the growing gloom.

So little cause for carolings
    Of such ecstatic sound
Was written on terrestrial things
    Afar or nigh around,
That I could think there trembled through
    His happy good-night air
Some blessed Hope, whereof he knew
    And I was unaware.

Now the Wolf is in the Cul-de-sac

WENDY PRATT

it's come down with the dusk, left
a vast geometry of pines, thin lines
of Christmas trees, sheep hemmed

into grey-black fields. It's worked
its way along the red brick walls,
PVC doors, nudged wind chimes
with its nose, paced the patios
and blanched itself to white in each
security light. You watch it coming,
your hands, like X-rays on the glass,
your face as undone
as an etch-a-sketch, and all
that keeps the wolf away is light.

So each house lights its windows;
kitchens bitten into squares,
bathrooms petalled-finger-prints
of oblique head shots over sinks.
The wolf leans up against
your letter box and presses
forward with the wind and while
the dog whines from the sofa,
wolf knows neither sit nor stay.

The Gardener's Daughter [extract]

ALFRED, LORD TENNYSON

And up we rose, and on the spur we went.

Not wholly in the busy world, nor quite
Beyond it, blooms the garden that I love.
News from the humming city comes to it
In sound of funeral or of marriage bells;
And, sitting muffled in dark leaves, you hear
The windy clanging of the minster clock;
Although between it and the garden lies

A league of grass, wash'd by a slow broad stream,
That, stirr'd with languid pulses of the oar,
Waves all its lazy lilies, and creeps on,
Barge-laden, to three arches of a bridge
Crown'd with the minster-towers.

The fields between
Are dewy-fresh, browsed by deep-udder'd kine,
And all about the large lime feathers low,
The lime a summer home of murmurous wings.

Dirty Bird

JANE BURN

Far from the sea, an obnoxious gull wakes me
with its insidious caw. It has moved inland
for easier pickings – dirty bird, go shit
on someone else's head. My hands brace
the bathroom sink – scabby piers, half immersed
in scum. A sagging chest spanned between,
suspension grown slack. When did I get so old?
The mirror is a taunt. No *fairest-of-them-all*
from my reflection, spotted with toothpaste,
like viewing myself through snow.

It has been a fortnight of slow dripping away.
I feel something, I feel nothing. Something,
nothing, nothing … *nothing*. I want to sleep
the clock around and see if you are still
around when I eventually wake.

Happiness

JANE KENYON

There's just no accounting for happiness,
or the way it turns up like a prodigal
who comes back to the dust at your feet
having squandered a fortune far away.

And how can you not forgive?
You make a feast in honor of what
was lost, and take from its place the finest
garment, which you saved for an occasion
you could not imagine, and you weep night and day
to know that you were not abandoned,
that happiness saved its most extreme form
for you alone.

No, happiness is the uncle you never
knew about, who flies a single-engine plane
onto the grassy landing strip, hitchhikes
into town, and inquires at every door
until he finds you asleep mid afternoon
as you so often are during the unmerciful
hours of your despair.

It comes to the monk in his cell.
It comes to the woman sweeping the street
with a birch broom, to the child
whose mother has passed out from drink.
It comes to the lover, to the dog chewing
a sock, to the pusher, to the basketmaker,
and to the clerk stacking cans of carrots
in the night.

      It even comes to the boulder
in the perpetual shade of pine barrens,
to rain falling on the open sea,
to the wineglass, weary of holding wine.

Poem

JONATHAN DAVIDSON

I wanted to cross the tidal river
by means of the ford the Romans found
and stumble up the shingle beach
to a new life on the northern shore.

And I wanted to have passed halfway,
midstream, drifting, a man heading south,
taking in water but likely to make it,
his heart set on seeing the turf maze

and buying a drink in the isolated pub.
And I will see him gather up my life
like a number of stacks of small change
stood on the mild- or bitter-puddled table.

Morning

CAROLINE YASUNAGA

The gentleness of secretaries in the morning is something
to behold. When they are arriving, fluttering through the
office and settling to their desks. They are cheery when
exchanging greetings and stories. I have noticed the
gentleness of secretaries before the day sets in and
before they are no longer available to themselves.

There are no gods

D. H. LAWRENCE

There are no gods, and you can please yourself
have a game of tennis, go out in the car, do some
   shopping, sit and talk, talk, talk
with a cigarette browning your fingers.

There are no gods, and you can please yourself –
go and please yourself –

But leave me alone, leave me alone, to myself!
and then in the room, whose is the presence
that makes the air so still and lovely to me?

Who is it that softly touches the sides of my breast
and touches me over the heart
so that my heart beats soothed, soothed, soothed and
   at peace?

Who is it smooths the bed-sheets like the cool
smooth ocean where the fishes rest on edge
in their own dream?

Who is it that clasps and kneads my naked feet, till they
    unfold,
till all is well, till all is utterly well? the lotus-lilies of the
    feet!

I tell you, it is no woman, it is no man, for I am alone.
And I fall asleep with the gods, the gods
that are not, or that are
according to the soul's desire,
like a pool into which we plunge, or do not plunge.

Song of Myself [extract]
WALT WHITMAN

Where the humming-bird shimmers, where the neck of
    the long-lived swan is curving and winding,
Where the laughing-gull scoots by the shore, where she
    laughs her near-human laugh,
Where bee-hives range on a gray bench in the garden
    half hid by the high weeds,

Where band-neck'd partridges roost in a ring on the
ground with their heads out,
Where burial coaches enter the arch'd gates of a
cemetery,
Where winter wolves bark amid wastes of snow and
icicled trees,
Where the yellow-crown'd heron comes to the edge of
the marsh at night and feeds upon small crabs,
Where the splash of swimmers and divers cools the
warm noon,
Where the katy-did works her chromatic reed on the
walnut-tree over the well,
Through patches of citrons and cucumbers with silver-
wired leaves,
Through the salt-lick or orange glade, or under conical
firs,
Through the gymnasium, through the curtain'd saloon,
through the office or public hall;
Pleas'd with the native and pleas'd with the foreign,
pleas'd with the new and old,
Pleas'd with the homely woman as well as the handsome,
Pleas'd with the quakeress as she puts off her bonnet and
talks melodiously,

Pleas'd with the tune of the choir of the whitewash'd
    church,
Pleas'd with the earnest words of the sweating Methodist
    preacher, impress'd seriously at the camp-meeting;
Looking in at the shop-windows of Broadway the whole
    forenoon, flatting the flesh of my nose on the thick
    plate glass,
Wandering the same afternoon with my face turn'd up to
    the clouds, or down a lane or along the beach,
My right and left arms round the sides of two friends,
    and I in the middle;
Coming home with the silent and dark-cheek'd bush-boy,
    (behind me he rides at the drape of the day)

Danse Russe

WILLIAM CARLOS WILLIAMS

If I when my wife is sleeping
and the baby and Kathleen
are sleeping
and the sun is a flame-white disc
in silken mists
above shining trees, –
if I in my north room
dance naked, grotesquely
before my mirror
waving my shirt round my head
and singing softly to myself:
'I am lonely, lonely.
I was born to be lonely,
I am best so!'
If I admire my arms, my face,
my shoulders, flanks, buttocks
again the yellow drawn shades, –

Who shall say I am not
the happy genius of my household?

On Living

NAZIM HIKMET

Translated by Mutlu Konuk and Randy Blasing

I.

Living is no laughing matter:

you must live with great seriousness

like a squirrel, for example –

I mean without looking for something beyond and above
      living,

I mean living must be your whole occupation.

Living is no laughing matter:

you must take it seriously,

so much so and to such a degree

that, for example, your hands tied behind your back,

your back to the wall,

or else in a laboratory

in your white coat and safety glasses,

you can die for people –

even for people whose faces you've never seen,

even though you know living

is the most real, the most beautiful thing.

I mean, you must take living so seriously

that even at seventy, for example, you'll plant olive trees –

and not for your children, either,
but because although you fear death you don't believe it,
because living, I mean, weighs heavier.

II.
Let's say we're seriously ill, need surgery –
which is to say we might not get up
from the white table.
Even though it's impossible not to feel sad
about going a little too soon,
we'll still laugh at the jokes being told,
we'll look out the window to see if it's raining,
or still wait anxiously
for the latest newscast …
Let's say we're at the front –
for something worth fighting for, say.
There, in the first offensive, on that very day,
we might fall on our face, dead.
We'll know this with a curious anger,
but we'll still worry ourselves to death
about the outcome of the war, which could last years.
Let's say we're in prison
and close to fifty,
and we have eighteen more years, say,

before the iron doors will open.
We'll still live with the outside,
with its people and animals, struggle and wind –
I mean with the outside beyond the walls.
I mean, however and wherever we are,
we must live as if we will never die.

III.
This earth will grow cold,
a star among stars
and one of the smallest,
a gilded mote on blue velvet –
I mean *this*, our great earth.
This earth will grow cold one day,
not like a block of ice
or a dead cloud even
but like an empty walnut it will roll along
in pitch-black space...
You must grieve for this right now
you have to feel this sorrow now –
for the world must be loved this much
if you're going to say 'I lived'...

Trust

D. H. LAWRENCE

Oh we've got to trust
one another again
in some essentials.

Not the narrow little
bargaining trust
that says: I'm for you
if you'll be for me. –

But a bigger trust,
a trust of the sun
that does not bother
about moth and rust,
and we see it shining
in one another.

Oh don't you trust me,
don't burden me
with your life and affairs; don't
thrust me
into your cares.

But I think you may trust
the sun in me
that glows with just
as much glow as you see
in me, and no more.

But if it warms
your heart's quick core
why then trust it, it forms
one faithfulness more.

And be, oh be
a sun to me,
not a weary, insistent
personality

but a sun that shines
and goes dark, but shines
again and entwines
with the sunshine in me

till we both of us
are more glorious
and more sunny.

Friday Afternoon

ALISON BRACKENBURY

It was the autumn's last day, when the roof
was skimmed by wings – Red Admiral butterfly? –
a glance of black against the sky, like truth.

It was on the day on which the goldfinch flung
its yellow wing against the glass, as though
it had drunk all the sweetness from the sun,

by which, in the wild garden, hips were seen
swelled by last night's rain, crowns under leaves,
as though they could stay glossy, ever green,

a day when children played and did not fall
when traffic stilled to world's edge, a gold crawl,
which I heard, sun-lapped, sleeping through it all.

O TASTE AND SEE

A few delicious poems on which to be
indulgent. They are full of good food
and coffee, figs and roses. I love Michelle
McGrane's way of looking at the world, her
delight in the sensuous and her belief in its
healing properties:

> Cure fatigue, insomnia or nightmares
> by boiling milk poured in a pail
> with sun-baked figs and turmeric.
> Add lavender honey to taste. Drink
> slowly.

I like to recommend them as a reminder
to enjoy life's small pleasures, so go ahead,
drink slowly …

Gloire de Dijon

D. H. LAWRENCE

When she rises in the morning
I linger to watch her;
She spreads the bath-cloth underneath the window
And the sunbeams catch her
Glistening white on the shoulders,
While down her sides the mellow
Golden shadow glows as
She stoops to the sponge, and her swung breasts
Sway like full-blown yellow
Gloire de Dijon roses.

She drips herself with water, and her shoulders
Glisten as silver, they crumple up
Like wet and falling roses, and I listen
For the sluicing of their rain-dishevelled petals.
In the window full of sunlight
Concentrates her golden shadow
Fold on fold, until it glows as
Mellow as the glory roses.

Thirteen Ways with Figs

MICHELLE McGRANE

1.

Silence the village gossip with nutty figs
rolled in crushed peppercorns.
Layer the fiery fruit in a jar between bay leaves.
Store in a dark place for three days.
Leave your offering on her doorstep.

2.

Sweeten your mother-in-law,
a small, crepey woman in a black dress
smelling of mothballs,
with stuffed quails roasted in thick balsamic sauce,
followed by ricotta-rose cheesecake and marzipan-filled figs.
Spill velvet-pink petals over her plate.

3.

Soothe inflamed ulcers and lesions
with a steamed fig, slippery elm, flaxseed poultice.
Wrap around the weeping skin in a muslin cloth.

4.

Pick a ribbed fig from the tree at twilight.
Split the dark cocoon in two.
Rub the wart with amber pulp and seeds.
Tie the halves together again.
Bury them in the flinty earth
under the waning moon.

5.

Cure fatigue, insomnia or nightmares
by boiling milk poured in a pail
with sun-baked figs and turmeric.
Add lavender honey to taste. Drink slowly.

6.

Bind three white Cilento figs
with a crimson ribbon for dreams of love.
Place the fruit under your pillow.
In the morning,
loop the ribbon around your waist.
If your heart is in your mouth,
sear it, eat it with figs.

7.

Beguile your partner with fig-leaf *absolute*
dabbed along the curve of your neck.
Wear almond blossoms in your hair.
Dance on a terrace with a view of the harbour,
to the flashing grin of an accordionist
who smells of sulphur and plays like the devil.
Clap your hands. This is no time to tiptoe.

8.

On a balmy midsummer evening, wrap up your *al fresco*
    meal
at the warped wooden table under the plane tree
with blistered grilled figs, spoonfuls of soft
    mascarpone
drizzled with orange blossom and rose water.
Smell the mimosa.
Don't wipe the sugary smudge from your chin.
Carry the sated silence to bed.

9.

Arouse your lover with plump, purple figs in a cool bowl
    of water.
Break the thin, moist skin with your fingers.
Close your eyes. Listen to your breathing.

10.

On a windy day welcome your new neighbours across
    the pasture.
Make them feel at home with *capocollo*,
a sausage of figs, almonds, pistachios and cinnamon.
Fold in leaves
left in a basket on the porch. Follow the dung
trail home, a wasp
hovering at your shoulder.

11.

In autumn, line your pantry shelves with jars of fig jam
scented with cardamom pods. Seal in the sunshine
with smooth wax discs and screw-top lids.

12.

Feed a hungry family
with slow-cooked pork loin and Adriatic fig stuffing.
Serve with golden polenta. Garnish with watercress.
Open bottles of the full bodied local wine.
Taste the olive-wood smoke,
the measure of November's indulgences.

13.

When the sky pops and hisses with stars,
celebrate the year's trailing tail.
Prepare fig fillets stuffed with amaretti *biscotti*
and smoky chocolate slivers.
Serve with steaming espressos before midnight.
Vabene.

Coffee in Heaven

JOHN AGARD

You'll be greeted
by a nice cup of coffee
when you get to heaven
and strains of angelic harmony.

But wouldn't you be devastated
if they only serve decaffeinated
while from the percolators of hell

your soul was assaulted
by Satan's fresh espresso smell?

Flight

LISA OLIVER

We breathe into sleep, the low rumble of rain on the roof,
the soft pulse of blood lullabying us.
Floor boards in our emptied house creak half-heard,

and I sink
into the hinterland, neither here nor there.

I wake to the thud of the newspaper, the gurgle of the
    heating.
I lie for a while. Half-remembered dreams scutter
back into the dark but the taste of them lingers
like salt on my tongue.

You are still sleeping so I creep down the stairs,
silence the kettle before it alarms you.
I hold the mug in my hands,
let it warm them.

I watch two summer-fat blackbirds breakfast on berries,
stripping the tree, whilst in the leaves,
a shoal of sparrows
dart and flash.

The dog races across morning-wet grass, high-fiving the
    day
he barks and dances a circle. The birds scatter
at the sound of him. I shield my eyes
as I watch them fly.

Hock and Soda-Water

LORD BYRON

Few things surpass old wine – and they may preach
   Who please (the more because they preach in vain),
Let us have wine and woman, mirth and laughter,
Sermons and soda-water the day after.

Man, being reasonable, must get drunk;
   The best of life is but intoxication:
Glory, the grape, love, gold – in these are sunk
The hopes of all men, and every nation;
But to return, get very drunk, and when
You wake with headache, you shall see what then.

Ring for your valet, bid him quickly bring
   Some hock and soda-water. Then you'll know
A pleasure worthy of Xerxes, the great king;
   For not the blest sherbet, sublimed with snow,
Nor the first sparkle in the desert spring,
   Nor Burgundy in all its sunset glow,
After long travel, ennui, love or slaughter,
Vie with that draught of hock and soda-water.

Fern Hill [extract]

DYLAN THOMAS

Now as I was young and easy under the apple boughs
About the lilting house and happy as the grass was green,
    The night above the dingle starry,
    Time let me hail and climb
    Golden in the heydays of his eyes,
And honoured among wagons I was prince of the apple
    towns
And once below a time I lordly had the trees and leaves
    Trail with daisies and barley
    Down the rivers of the windfall light.

And as I was green and carefree, famous among the
    barns
About the happy yard and singing as the farm was home,
    In the sun that is young once only,
    Time let me play and be
    Golden in the mercy of his means,
And green and golden I was huntsman and herdsman,
    the calves
Sang to my horn, the foxes on the hills barked clear and
    cold,

And the sabbath rang slowly
In the pebbles of the holy streams.

Ice on the Highway

THOMAS HARDY

Seven buxom women abreast, and arm in arm,
    Trudge down the hill, tip-toed,
    And breathing warm;
They must perforce trudge thus, to keep upright
    On the glassy ice-bound road,

And they must get to market whether or no,
    Provisions running low
    With the nearing Saturday night,
While the lumbering van wherein they mostly ride
    Can nowise go:
Yet loud their laughter as they stagger and slide!

The Fired Pot

ANNA WICKHAM

In our town, people live in rows.
The only irregular thing in a street is the steeple;
And where that points to, God only knows,
And not the poor disciplined people!

And I have watched the women growing old,
Passionate about pins, and pence, and soap,
Till the heart within my wedded breast grew cold,
And I lost hope.

But a young soldier came to our town,
He spoke his mind most candidly.
He asked me quickly to lie down,
And that was very good for me.

For though I gave him no embrace –
Remembering my duty –
He altered the expression of my face,
And gave me back my beauty.

Summer Holidays

MEG COX

Me and my friends
did a lot of poking about
in a desultory kind of a way
for weeks, it seemed like.

Sometimes we went
as far as 'the dam'
which wasn't one
any more.

Everywhere was covered
in wild garlic.

Sometimes we went
to the pine wood forest
where we had a den
and showed each other
our bottoms.
Maybe that was just once.

Sometimes we looked

for adders and found
grass snakes.

Sometimes we sat
in hedges and
didn't do anything much.

O Taste and See

DENISE LEVERTOV

The world is
not with us enough
O taste and see

the subway Bible poster said,
meaning The Lord, meaning
if anything all that lives
to the imagination's tongue,

grief, mercy, language,
tangerine, weather, to

breathe them, bite,
savor, chew, swallow, transform

into our flesh our
deaths, crossing the street, plum, quince,
living in the orchard and being

hungry, and plucking
the fruit.

Delight in Disorder

ROBERT HERRICK

A sweet disorder in the dress
Kindles in clothes a wantonness;
A lawn about the shoulders thrown
Into a fine distraction;
An erring lace, which here and there
Enthrals the crimson stomacher;
A cuff neglectful, and thereby
Ribands to flow confusedly;

A winning wave, deserving note,
In the tempestuous petticoat;
A careless shoe-string, in whose tie
I see a wild civility:
Do more bewitch me, than when art
Is too precise in every part.

The washing never gets done

I believe that there is a part of each of us that is a poet: the part that is capable of stopping to appreciate the beautiful and the marvellous in the stuff of the everyday.

They are all a sacrament of the mundane, a kind of prayerfulness that is found in the repetition of small acts: the washing of wine glasses, lighting lamps and fires, small services of love. In the case of Steve Harrison's poem, he mourns the things he never had.

The poems in this section answer James Sheard's question:

tell me what these things were
and why it was they mattered.

Wine Glasses

JEFF PHELPS

Wine glasses must be washed first
in water hot as hands can bear, untainted
by the everyday of cutlery and plates.
Rub out the deep red lees, invert them,
stems-up to stand like potters' kilns.
I think I had forgotten what a poem was
till you reminded me how the world can be made
to scintillate on a single wavelength.
Now I hold the glass up to the light.
The taut brittle arc of its bowl is faith
in the impossible. I rub a moist finger round the rim,
hear a kind of gathering, a resonance that's neither
glass nor air, but a new place between.
Its high sound fills the kitchen like a prayer bell.

Poem for People That Are Understandably too Busy to Read Poetry

STEPHEN DUNN

Relax. This won't last long.
Or if it does, or if the lines
make you sleepy or bored,
give in to sleep, turn on
the TV, deal the cards.
This poem is built to withstand
such things. Its feelings
cannot be hurt. They exist
somewhere in the poet,
and I am far away.
Pick it up anytime. Start it
in the middle if you wish.
It is as approachable as melodrama,
and can offer you violence
if it is violence you like. Look,
there's a man on a sidewalk;
the way his leg is quivering
he'll never be the same again.
This is your poem
and I know you're busy at the office

or the kids are into your last nerve.
Maybe it's sex you've always wanted.
Well, they lie together
like the party's unbuttoned coats,
slumped on the bed
waiting for drunken arms to move them.
I don't think you want me to go on;
everyone has his expectations, but this
is a poem for the entire family.
Right now, Budweiser
is dripping from a waterfall,
deodorants are hissing into armpits
of people you resemble,
and the two lovers are dressing now,
saying farewell.
I don't know what music this poem
can come up with, but clearly
it's needed. For it's apparent
they will never see each other again
and we need music for this
because there was never music when he or she
left you standing on the corner.
You see, I want this poem to be nicer
than life. I want you to look at it

when anxiety zigzags your stomach
and the last tranquilizer is gone
and you need someone to tell you
I'll be here when you want me
like the sound inside a shell.
The poem is saying that to you now.
But don't give anything for this poem.
It doesn't expect much. It will never say more
than listening can explain.
Just keep it in your attache case
or in your house. And if you're not asleep
by now, or bored beyond sense,
the poem wants you to laugh. Laugh at
yourself, laugh at this poem, at all poetry.
Come on:

Good. Now here's what poetry can do.

Imagine yourself a caterpillar.
There's an awful shrug and, suddenly,
You're beautiful for as long as you live.

Baby Running Barefoot

D. H. LAWRENCE

When the bare feet of the baby beat across the grass
The little white feet nod like white flowers in the wind,
They poise and run like ripples lapping across the water:
And the sight of their white playing in the grass
Is like a little robin's song, winsome,
Or as two white butterflies that settle in the cup of one
    flower
For a moment, then away with a flutter of wings.

I long for the baby to wander hither to me
Like a wind-shadow wandering over the water,
So that she can stand on my knee
With her little bare feet in my hands,
Cool like syringa buds,
Firm and silken like young peony flowers.

On Hearing for the First Time

CAROLE BROMLEY

'It sounds very very high'

and she sobs for the joy of it,
for the reds and blues of it,
the shock, the hullabaloo,

the kerfuffle, the Sturm und Drang,
the sudden ice cream in a shake,
the sherbet firework burst.

'It's just amazing' she cries
her face in her hands.
'I'm going to say the months of the year'

and she hears them, shaking,
'January February March'
April overwhelms her.

It's like never having seen a bird,
or the sea or the stars
never tasting an orange,

like living all your life in a cave
and coming out into the light,
the sun on your face.

Afterwards she walks by the Tyne,
daren't go alone for fear
the birdsong, the traffic, the ship's hooter

will be too much. They are not.
It's like falling in love.

My Mother's Bathroom Armoury

JACQUELINE SAPHRA

Beehive proppers backcomb teasers
Pinpoint pluck of fearful tweezers
Leak of mouthwash morbid flavour
Dutch-cap dusted snap-shut cover
Cutting edge of lady-razor
Glint of sin and lure of danger
Woman's flesh a fading treasure
Braced for pain but honed for pleasure

Caked on flakes of failed concealer
Tell-tale cheeks of blusher-stealer
Crimson smear of lipstick wearer
Smile expander mouth preparer
Burning bleach a making-over
Smudged remains of caked mascara
Iron clamp of eyelash curler
Usual instruments of torture
Bath brimful of scented water
Mother's tricks will pass to daughter

This year next year sometime never

Bed in Summer

ROBERT LOUIS STEVENSON

In winter I get up at night
And dress by yellow candle-light.
In summer, quite the other way,
I have to go to bed by day.

I have to go to bed and see
The birds still hopping on the tree,
Or hear the grown-up people's feet
Still going past me in the street.

And does it not seem hard to you,
When all the sky is clear and blue,
And I should like so much to play,
To have to go to bed by day?

Tides

HUGO WILLIAMS

The evening advances, then withdraws again
Leaving our cups and books like islands on the floor.
We are drifting you and I,
As far from one another as the young heroes
Of these two novels we have just laid down.
For that is happiness: to wander alone
Surrounded by the same moon, whose tides remind us of
    ourselves,

Our distances, and what we leave behind.
The lamp left on, the curtains letting in the light.
These things were promises. No doubt we will come
    back to them.

The washing never gets done

JAAN KAPLINSKI

Translated from the Estonian by Jaan Kaplinski, with Sam
Hamill and Runa Tamm

The washing never gets done.
The furnace never gets heated.
Books never get read.
Life is never completed.
Life is like a ball which one must continually
catch and hit so that it won't fall.
When the fence is repaired at one end,
it collapses at the other. The roof leaks,
the kitchen door won't close, there are cracks in the
    foundation,
the torn knees of children's pants…

One can't keep everything in mind. The wonder is
that beside all this one can notice
the spring which is so full of everything
continuing in all directions – into evening clouds,
into the redwing's song and into every
drop of dew on every blade of grass in the meadow,
as far as the eye can see, into the dusk.

Tŷ Unnos (One Night House)

LESLEY INGRAM

Sunrise, the things I offer you:
a house coughed up overnight
by the earth in its own image,
gorse, sods, turf, an eyeful

of window facing sunwards,
an open door, a dirt floor
to be polished by the weight
of dancing feet and babies' knees,

a hearth in full flame, smoke
surprised and blinking
through hazel wicker,
a chimney, triumphant.

My back into everything.
The *cwtch* in my arms.
The trajectory of an axe,
the distance it yields. Years.

My Mother's Arts

THIRZA CLOUT

My mother was an alchemist, she conjured
magic from Dettol ointment and Lucozade.
At the first sniff bruises faded, grazes healed.

With silver instruments she cut holy strips
from a reel to seal squares of gauze. When
measles or a bilious attack struck one of us

she was at her best, no good hidings given
nor tears before bedtime threatened. Instead
mother ascended bearing the bottle to the bedside

of the fortunate child, crackled back cellophane,
poured out gold. I hid from her with great cunning
my worst wound, scrawled mute hieroglyphs
and in silence nursed a burning stone.

The Tom-Cat

DON MARQUIS

At midnight in the alley
A tom-cat comes to wail,
And he chants the hate of a million years
As he swings his snaky tail.

Malevolent, bony, brindled,
Tiger and devil and bard,
His eyes are coals from the middle of Hell
And his heart is black and hard.

He twists and crouches and capers
And bares his curved sharp claws,
And he sings to the stars of the jungle nights
Ere cities were, or laws.

Beast from a world primeval,
He and his leaping clan,
When the blotched red moon leers over the roofs
Give voice to their scorn of man.

He will lie on a rug to-morrow
And lick his silky fur,
And veil the brute in his yellow eyes
And play he's tame, and purr.

But at midnight in the alley
He will crouch again and wail,
And beat the time for his demon's song
With the swing of his demon's tail.

One Day a Student Called me 'Dad'

STEVE HARRISON

A slip of some sort; sleepless or Freudian.
I asked what we were having for tea that night,
'Beans' his quick, canned reply.
A table set for three maybe more.

Mantle piece altered with Father's cards
of boats, steam trains, cricket, ironic pipes.
A bellows and family of coordinated poker, brush, tongs
companion set in the fireplace below.
Places I'd never been on the fridge in a clumsy
magnetic gallery of unknown adventures.
A dozen fish fingers' clockwork face in the frying pan.

A shed-full of wrongly angled bikes;
workshop for rites of passage until
young greasy thumbs were strong enough to re-fit
punctured tyres back over the wheel rim
without my help, or trapping the snaking inner tube;
fellow conspirator to sneak out
clean bowls of still water

from banned hygienic kitchens,
looking for giveaway bubbles.

The end of school day bell went.
All was packed-up, desk cleared.

A table unset for one awaited.

Those Winter Sundays

ROBERT HAYDEN

Sundays too my father got up early
and put his clothes on in the blueblack cold,
then with cracked hands that ached
from labor in the weekday weather made
banked fires blaze. No one ever thanked him.

I'd wake and hear the cold splintering, breaking.
When the rooms were warm, he'd call,
and slowly I would rise and dress,
fearing the chronic angers of that house,

Speaking indifferently to him,
who had driven out the cold
and polished my good shoes as well.
What did I know, what did I know
of love's austere and lonely offices?

Our London Underground

FRASER SOUTHEY

April morning, rain first thing
and as she turns towards me,
nightdress twisted tight above her waist,
I learn again her scars and stretch marks,
which she makes no move to hide

so I smile and say –
they make the Central Line,
follow their mercury threads,
whisper – *Stratford East to Ruislip West,*
she laughs,

strokes the veins
worming their way across my thighs,
see you have them too –
Northern – Jubilee – Bakerloo.
I shift on to my back,

she twists a crazed hair from my gut –
signal delays – Ealing Broadway.
I steer her hand towards my groin in jest –
the next stop will be Monument.
We laugh again, then sleep,

no kids at home to hear our snores
above the horns and sirens
on the roaring streets.

Cargo Cult

JAMES SHEARD

In an imperfect incense
of soil and old candles

the kept objects sit
on split grey shelving –
dull cones of lead, broken tools,
bits of strange bracketry.

For a while I fake
the slimfingered expertise
of a collector turning porcelain,
before letting my square hands
hang and rust.

Tumbled here like cargo
from the metal perfection
of a distant father, pinning me
between fool and acolyte,

between turning and waiting
a quiet unscowling moment longer
for him to return

and tell me what these things were
and why it was they mattered.

Wind

TED HUGHES

This house has been far out at sea all night,
The woods crashing through darkness, the booming hills,
Winds stampeding the fields under the window
Floundering black astride and blinding wet

Till day rose; then under an orange sky
The hills had new places, and wind wielded
Blade-light, luminous black and emerald,
Flexing like the lens of a mad eye.

At noon I scaled along the house-side as far as
The coal-house door. Once I looked up –
Through the brunt wind that dented the balls of my eyes
The tent of the hills drummed and strained its guyrope,

The fields quivering, the skyline a grimace,
At any second to bang and vanish with a flap;
The wind flung a magpie away and a black-
Back gull bent like an iron bar slowly. The house

Rang like some fine green goblet in the note
That any second would shatter it. Now deep
In chairs, in front of the great fire, we grip
Our hearts and cannot entertain book, thought,

Or each other. We watch the fire blazing,
And feel the roots of the house move, but sit on,
Seeing the window tremble to come in,
Hearing the stones cry out under the horizons.

LET ME COUNT THE WAYS

There are very many different ways of loving: unrequited love, unsuitable love, lost love, tender love, and how love can play tricks. This chapter deals with all of these, and more.

Please can I have a man

SELIMA HILL

Please can I have a man who wears corduroy.
Please can I have a man
who knows the names of 100 different roses;
who doesn't mind my absent-minded rabbits
wandering in and out
as if they own the place,
who makes me creamy curries from fresh lemongrass,

who walks like Belmondo in *A Bout de Souffle*;
who sticks all my carefully-selected postcards –
sent from exotic cities
he doesn't expect to come with me to,
but would if I asked, which I will do –
with nobody else's, up his bedroom wall,
starting with Ivy, the Famous Diving Pig,

whose picture, in action, I bought ten copies of;
who talks like Belmondo too, with lips as smooth
and tightly-packed as chocolate-coated
(melting chocolate) peony buds;
who knows that piling himself drunkenly on top of me

like a duvet stuffed with library books and shopping bags
is very easy: please can I have a man

who is not prepared to do that.
Who is not prepared to say I'm pretty either.
Who, when I come trotting in from the bathroom
like a squealing freshly-scrubbed piglet
that likes nothing better than a binge
of being affectionate and undisciplined and uncomplicated,
opens his arms like a trough for me to dive into.

Reconciliation

ELSE LASKER-SCHULER

Translated from the German by James Sheard

Into my lap, a great star will fall…
we would keep watch at night,

praying in languages
carved like harps.

We would make our peace with the night –
so much of God flows through it.

Our hearts are like children,
wanting sleepsweet rest.

And our lips want to kiss,
so what makes you hold back?

Does my heart not border on yours,
your blood not redden my cheek?

We would make our peace with the night,
and if we embrace, we will not die.

Into my lap, a great star will fall.

A Glimpse

WALT WHITMAN

A glimpse through an interstice caught,
Of a crowd of workmen and drivers in a bar-room
　　around the stove late of a winter night, and I
　　unremark'd seated in a corner,
Of a youth who loves me and whom I love, silently
　　approaching and seating himself near, that he may
　　hold me by the hand,
A long while amid the noises of coming and going, of
　　drinking and oath and smutty jest,
There we two, content, happy in being together, speaking
　　little, perhaps not a word.

The Good-Morrow

JOHN DONNE

I wonder, by my troth, what thou and I
Did, till we loved? Were we not weaned till then?
But sucked on country pleasures, childishly?

Or snorted we in the Seven Sleepers' den?
'Twas so; but this, all pleasures fancies be.
If ever any beauty I did see,
Which I desired, and got, 'twas but a dream of thee.

And now good-morrow to our waking souls,
Which watch not one another out of fear;
For love, all love of other sights controls,
And makes one little room an everywhere.
Let sea-discoverers to new worlds have gone,
Let maps to other, worlds on worlds have shown,
Let us possess one world, each hath one, and is one.

My face in thine eye, thine in mine appears,
And true plain hearts do in the faces rest;
Where can we find two better hemispheres,
Without sharp north, without declining west?
Whatever dies, was not mixed equally;
If our two loves be one, or, thou and I
Love so alike, that none do slacken, none can die.

Canoe

KEITH DOUGLAS

Well, I am thinking this may be my last
summer, but cannot lose even a part
of pleasure in the old-fashioned art
of idleness. I cannot stand aghast

at whatever doom hovers in the background:
while grass and buildings and the somnolent river,
who know they are allowed to last forever,
exchange between them the whole subdued sound

of this hot time. What sudden fearful fate
can deter my shade wandering next year
from a return? Whistle and I will hear
and come again another evening, when this boat

travels with you alone toward Iffley:
as you lie looking up for thunder again,
this cool touch does not betoken rain;
it is my spirit that kisses your mouth lightly.

Summer with Monika

ROGER McGOUGH

ten milk bottles standing in the hall
ten milk bottles up against the wall
next door neighbour thinks we're dead
hasn't heard a sound, he said
doesn't know we've been in bed
the ten whole days since we were wed
no-one knows and no-one sees
we lovers doing as we please
but people stop and point at these
ten milk bottles a-turning into cheese

ten milk bottles standing day and night
ten different thicknesses and
different shades of white
persistent carol singers without a note to utter
silent carol singers a-turning into butter

now she's run out of passion
and there's not much left in me
so maybe we'll get up and make a cup of tea
and then people can stop wondering

what they're waiting for
those ten milk bottles a queuing at our door
those ten milk bottles a queuing at our door.

Sonnet 130

WILLIAM SHAKESPEARE

My mistress' eyes are nothing like the sun;
Coral is far more red than her lips' red;
If snow be white, why then her breasts are dun;
If hairs be wires, black wires grow on her head.
I have seen roses damasked, red and white,
But no such roses see I in her cheeks;
And in some perfumes is there more delight
Than in the breath that from my mistress reeks.
I love to hear her speak, yet well I know
That music hath a far more pleasing sound;
I grant I never saw a goddess go;
My mistress when she walks treads on the ground.
    And yet, by heaven, I think my love as rare
    As any she belied with false compare.

Kisses

THOMAS CAMPION

My Love bound me with a kiss
That I should no longer stay.
When I felt so sweet a bliss,
I had less power to pass away.
Alas! that women do not know
Kisses make men loth to go.

Yes, she knows it but too well,
For I heard when Venus' dove
In her ear did softly tell
That kisses were the seals of love.
O! muse not then though it be so,
Kisses make men loth to go.

Wherefore did she thus inflame
My desires, heat my blood,
Instantly to quench the same,
And starve whom she had given food?
I the common sense can show;
Kisses make men loth to go.

Had she bid me go at first,
It would ne'er have grieved my heart;
Hope delayed had been the worst.
But ah! to kiss and then to part!
How deep it struck, speak, gods, you know.
Kisses make men loth to go.

Sonnet 43

ELIZABETH BARRETT BROWNING

How do I love thee? Let me count the ways.
I love thee to the depth and breadth and height
My soul can reach, when feeling out of sight
For the ends of being and ideal grace.
I love thee to the level of every day's
Most quiet need, by sun and candle-light.
I love thee freely, as men strive for right.
I love thee purely, as they turn from praise.
I love thee with the passion put to use
In my old griefs, and with my childhood's faith.
I love thee with a love I seemed to lose

With my lost saints. I love thee with the breath,
Smiles, tears, of all my life; and, if God choose,
I shall but love thee better after death.

The Light Beneath

ANGELA FRANCE

She looks up from the potatoes, sees him in the garden
and watches as he levels a molehill. He spreads earth
over the border, scrapes the ground flat, bends
to dust off a low leaf. She knows he will clean
his spade, wash his hands and leave his boots
in the mud room before he comes to sit at the table
and wait behind his newspaper for lunch.

Friends ask how she copes with his dour silence.
She could tell them how he's got up first for thirty years
to make the coffee, how he's always folded
his warm legs around her feet on winter nights,
how the first blooms of summer are cut for the kitchen
table before she knows they exist. She couldn't explain

how once, when she was ill, she woke to find him
watching over her, hollow faced.

She sees he's flattening another mound as a neighbour
stops to talk. She can see the man is animated,
fast-talking, pointing and making sharp stabs
in the air. She can guess that he offers suggestions
of poison or traps. She doesn't need to hear her husband
to know what he says as he turns away,
she's heard it before: *They lighten the soil.*

Sonnet 18

WILLIAM SHAKESPEARE

Shall I compare thee to a summer's day?
Thou art more lovely and more temperate.
Rough winds do shake the darling buds of May,
And summer's lease hath all too short a date.
Sometime too hot the eye of heaven shines,
And often is his gold complexion dimmed;
And every fair from fair sometime declines,

By chance, or nature's changing course, untrimmed;
But thy eternal summer shall not fade,
Nor lose possession of that fair thou ow'st,
Nor shall death brag thou wand'rest in his shade,
When in eternal lines to Time thou grow'st.
    So long as men can breathe, or eyes can see,
    So long lives this, and this gives life to thee.

I Loved You

ALEXANDER PUSHKIN

Translated by D. Zhuravlev

I loved you; even now I may confess
Some embers of my love their fire retain
But do not let it cause you more distress –
I do not want to sadden you again.
Hopeless and tongue-tied, yet, I loved you dearly
With pangs the jealous and the timid know
So tenderly I loved you, so sincerely,
I pray God grant another love you so.

The Doubtful Season

SIDNEY KEYES

The doubtful season of the brain's black weather
Blew through me, but you waited for its end.
My months were all named backwards till you showed me
That even the mind is not deceived for ever.

O in October it would be the blazoned
Leaves of the chestnut on the cobbled pavement:
And we would seek in the corridors of autumn
Denial of faith and of the summer's achievement.

And in the early year it was another
Sign of evasion when the poplars clattered
To sharpened ears above the metal river –
And I would turn to find your eyes were shuttered.

Even that almost parting on the stair
I could not understand, nor why the candles
Sprouted such flowers between our sculptured faces:
Nor why the river glinted in your hair.

O in July it was our love was started

Like any hare among the watchful grasses;
Its running is my song, my only song
How time turns back and the doubtful season passes.

Sonnet XLIII

EDNA ST. VINCENT MILLAY

What lips my lips have kissed, and where, and why,
I have forgotten, and what arms have lain
Under my head till morning; but the rain
Is full of ghosts tonight, that tap and sigh
Upon the glass and listen for reply,
And in my heart there stirs a quiet pain
For unremembered lads that not again
Will turn to me at midnight with a cry.
Thus in winter stands the lonely tree,
Nor knows what birds have vanished one by one,
Yet knows its boughs more silent than before:
I cannot say what loves have come and gone,
I only know that summer sang in me
A little while, that in me sings no more.

La Belle Dame Sans Merci: A Ballad [extract]

JOHN KEATS

I met a lady in the meads,
    Full beautiful – a faery's child,
Her hair was long, her foot was light,
    And her eyes were wild.

I made a garland for her head,
    And bracelets too, and fragrant zone;
She looked at me as she did love,
And made sweet moan.

I set her on my pacing steed,
    And nothing else saw all day long,
For sidelong would she bend, and sing
    A faery's song.

She found me roots of relish sweet,
    And honey wild, and manna-dew,
And sure in language strange she said –
    'I love thee true.'

She took me to her elfin grot,

And there she wept and sighed full sore,
And there I shut her wild wild eyes
    With kisses four.

And there she lullèd me asleep,
    And there I dreamed – Ah! woe betide! –
The latest dream I ever dreamt
    On the cold hill side.

Spilt

JEAN SPRACKLAND

You took handfuls of sea
to fill the moat of your brother's castle.
First you ran, then went low and steady,
but still it spilt. And you
didn't see this as the fault of the water,
its special talent for escape. To you
this was one more failure
to be shaken off with the weight of childhood.
You shaped the bowl of your hands,

pressed your fingers together,
held it against the sun to check the seal,
crouched in the shallows,
scooped again, again.

And here you are, going low and steady
between your two lives, walking
the impossible street that connects them.
It's dusk. A neighbour
setting bottles on her doorstep
throws you a foreign glance.
And still you arrive
with nothing to offer the people you love
but damp fingers, the evidence.

He Wishes for the Cloths of Heaven

WILLIAM BUTLER YEATS

Had I the heavens' embroidered cloths,
Enwrought with golden and silver light,
The blue and the dim and the dark cloths

Of night and light and the half-light,
I would spread the cloths under your feet:
But I, being poor, have only my dreams;
I have spread my dreams under your feet;
Tread softly because you tread on my dreams.

On My First Son

BEN JONSON

Farewell, thou child of my right hand, and joy;
My sin was too much hope of thee, lov'd boy.
Seven years tho' wert lent to me, and I thee pay,
Exacted by thy fate, on the just day.
O, could I lose all father now! For why
Will man lament the state he should envy?
To have so soon 'scap'd world's and flesh's rage,
And if no other misery, yet age?
Rest in soft peace, and, ask'd, say, 'Here doth lie
Ben Jonson his best piece of poetry.'
For whose sake henceforth all his vows be such,
As what he loves may never like too much.

Morning Song

SYLVIA PLATH

Love set you going like a fat gold watch.
The midwife slapped your footsoles, and your bald cry
Took its place among the elements.

Our voices echo, magnifying your arrival. New statue.
In a drafty museum, your nakedness
Shadows our safety. We stand round blankly as walls.

I'm no more your mother
Than the cloud that distills a mirror to reflect its own slow
Effacement at the wind's hand.

All night your moth-breath
Flickers among the flat pink roses. I wake to listen:
A far sea moves in my ear.

One cry, and I stumble from bed, cow-heavy and floral
In my Victorian nightgown.
Your mouth opens clean as a cat's. The window square

Whitens and swallows its dull stars. And now you try

Your handful of notes;
The clear vowels rise like balloons.

When all the others were away at Mass

SEAMUS HEANEY

When all the others were away at Mass
I was all hers as we peeled potatoes.
They broke the silence, let fall one by one
Like solder weeping off the soldering iron:
Cold comforts set between us, things to share
Gleaming in a bucket of clean water.
And again let fall. Little pleasant splashes
From each other's work would bring us to our senses.

So while the parish priest at her bedside
Went hammer and tongs at the prayers for the dying
And some were responding and some crying
I remembered her head bent towards my head,
Her breath in mine, our fluent dipping knives –
Never closer the whole rest of our lives.

Somewhat Unravelled

JO SHAPCOTT

Auntie stands by the kettle, looking at the kettle
and says, help me, where is the kettle?
I say, little auntie, the curlicues and hopscotch grids
unfurling in your brain have hidden it from you. Let me
make you a cup of tea. She says ah ha! but I do
my crossword, don't I, OK not the difficult one, the one
with the wasname? Cryptic clues. Not that. I say
auntie, little auntie, we were never very cryptic
so let's not start now. I appreciate your straight-on talk,
the built-up toilet seats, the way you wish poetry
were just my hobby, our cruises on the stair lift,
your concern about my weight, the special seat in the bath.
We know where we are. She says, nurse told me I
should furniture-walk around the house, holding on to it.
I say, little auntie you are a plump armchair
in flight, a kitchen table on a difficult hike without boots,
you do the sideboard crawl like no one else, you are a sofa
rumba, you go to sleep like a rug. She says,
I don't like eating. Just as well *you've* got
a good appetite. I say littlest auntie, my very little auntie
(because she is shrinking now, in front of me)

let me cook for you, a meal so wholesome and blimmin'
pungent with garlic you will dance on it and
eat it through your feet. Then she says don't you
ever want to go to market and get lost
in pots, fruit and random fabric? Don't you
want to experiment with rain, hide out in storms,
cover your body with a layer only one raindrop
thick? Don't you want to sell your nail-clippings
online? She says, look at you, with all your language,
you never became the flower your mother
wanted but it's not too late, come with me
and rootle in the earth outside my front window,
set yourself in the special bed, the one only
wasname is allowed to garden and we will practise
opening and closing and we'll follow the sun
with our faces until the cows come home.

Washing My Mother's Hair
CHAR MARCH

She's bird-thin,
fragile as her brittle smile,
her teeth suddenly too big for her mouth
lips thinned, clumsy with Vaseline
to stop the cracks showing.

Only last summer she broke
the world record in Running For The Bus
carrier bags thumping at her varicose legs
then fanned herself with the *Radio Times*
all the fifteen stops home.

Now her spine is hooked
into a question mark
from which her head tries to look up.
She doesn't have to bend at all to get her hair
into the wash-basin.

For the first time in my life,
and hers, I pour the warm water,
the baby shampoo, the best conditioner I could buy,

rub the blushing whiteness of her scalp gently
while she holds her flannel

clamped to her eyes like she taught me to.
And she says *Oh that's lovely. Just what I need.*
That's right, give it a good rub. Oh that's just lovely.
Sure and I'll be a new woman.
And I rub and chat quietly

and joke with her in a put-on voice:
Has Madam done her numbers for the lottery yet?
and *Will it be Torremolinos again this year, Madam?*
and the other things that mind-numbed hairdressers
say to their ladies.

And nothing at all
about how much
I love her.

The Pale Horse

LESLEY INGRAM

At twilight she is still sitting with the book in her hand,
staring through the window, looking for snow.

Have you seen my horse? she says, eyes wild
with loss. I smile, brush her hair. She purrs.

She cups my face. *I know you,* she whispers,
have you stolen my horse? I cover her hands with mine

and we stare a while, nose to nose. *I know you.*
Her lips twitch, try to find the forgotten shape

of my name. I tell her, but she shrugs and turns
to the window, expecting snow.

Summertime

after Chris Powici

MAGGIE MACKAY

My mother is clearing dandelions
in the rockery at the front of the house.
Trowel in hand, she has just rocked back
to greet a neighbour on the street
who waits by the gate for a blether.
Soon she will come through the open door,
to pour tea and watch *The Chase*.
But for now she walks down the stone path,
her hair bleached by days of sun.
So I imagine.

Under the Lemon Tree

MARSHA DE LA O

Not rain, but fine mist
falls from my lemon tree,
a balm of droplets in green shadow.

Six years now my mother gone to earth.
This dew, light as footsteps of the dead.
She often walked out here, craned her neck,
considered the fruit, hundreds of globes
in their leathery hides, figuring on
custard and pudding, meringue and
hollandaise.

But her plans didn't work out.

The tree goes on unceasingly – lemons fall
and fold into earth and begin again –
me, I come here as a salve against heat,
come to languish, to let the soft bursts –
essence of citrus, summer's distillate –
drift into my face and settle. Water and gold
brew in the quiet deeps at the far end

of the season. Leaves swallow the body
of light and the breath of water brims over.

My hands cup each other the way hers did.

Kitchen Ghosts

ANGELA TOPPING

Steps echo on terracotta tiles
but no-one's there.

In the morning
someone's washed the pots,
left them gleaming
piled high
in a white china mountain.
The drainer's neat,
a small cloth wrung out,
draped over the tap.
Crumbs have been
brushed up. On scrubbed table

one empty tea mug stands.
Father's mug. Always
drank his tea black.
That's how I know.

I can see his workaday hands
never tiring of setting things straight.

He is expecting Mother,
wonders when she'll come.
Each morning, I hope for
lemon drizzle cake, two
pieces missing,
two empty cups.

Four Years Later

PAMELA GILLILAN

The smell of him went soon
from all his shirts.
I sent them for jumble,

and the sweaters and suits.
The shoes
held more of him; he was printed
into his shoes. I did not burn
or throw or give them away.
Time has denatured them now.

Nothing left.
There will never be
a hair of his in a comb.
But I want to believe
that in the shifting housedust
minute presences still drift:
an eyelash,
a hard crescent cut from a fingernail,
that sometimes
between the folds of a curtain
or the covers of a book
I touch
a flake of his skin.

The bustle in a house

EMILY DICKINSON

The bustle in a house
The morning after death
Is solemnest of industries
Enacted upon earth, –

The sweeping up the heart,
And putting love away
We shall not want to use again
Until eternity.

Elegy

in memoriam SKK

SIDNEY KEYES

April again, and it's a year again
Since you walked out and slammed the door
Leaving us tangled in your words. Your brain
Lives in the bank-book and your eyes look up

Laughing from the carpet on the floor:
And we still drink from your silver cup.

It is a year again since they poured
The dumb ground into your mouth:
And yet we know, by some recurring word
Or look caught unawares, that you still drive
Our thoughts like the smart cobs of your youth –
When you and the world were alive.

A year again, and we have fallen on bad times
Since they gave you to the worms.
I am ashamed to take delight in these rhymes
Without grief; but you need no tears.
We shall never forget nor escape you, nor make terms
With your enemies, the swift departing years.

The Sound of a Knot Being Untied

ANGELA READMAN

Look to your lasses, lads, if you can, pull away
and fold paper to slip under the cracket leg
on the clackety slate. Fingers slick with the art
of her spit, she shushes out lamps, climbs the stairs
and flaps into a nightdress before the candle is lit.
I don't know when being naked stopped being simple,
if I stopped trying to catch her bathe, raindrops
falling, hung on the clothes line as the water
rolled, anchored a collar bone. It snowed all winter
when I wed, moths beat at windows, my shy wife
balling herself into bed to pull the eiderdown
ower her head, the pale of her spilt ower, out
onto cottage roofs, loud grass, hoof prints fleeced silent.
I can't see how I got to tonight, flickers of a woman
at our window. She lets go of a small sigh, frost
scratches feathers to the glass and the wind lifts
brown leaves up, upping like soaped leather shoes
dancing out of the yard. Look at it, lads, all of it,
now, listen to slow combs of hair, a strand flying
to horsehair bright as lightning over the dunes,
a click of her ring on oak as she scrapes off soap,

unknots a handkerchief and slips it over the silver
sly as cloud across a moon. Look to that lass now
a mouthful of sorrys opened, and kiss her while you can.[1]

---

1. According to legend, some women could raise the wind
or prevent storms at sea by tying knots in a handkerchief in a
particular way. Fishermen carried such knotted handkerchiefs
for a safe voyage.

It feels like going home

These poems are unified by the mystery of memory, nostalgia, homecoming and mortality. They are often in a minor key, ranging from beautiful to sad to hopeful.

> I have been here before,
> But when or how I cannot tell;
> I know the grass beyond the door,
> The sweet keen smell

Strawberries

EDWIN MORGAN

There were never strawberries
like the ones we had
that sultry afternoon
sitting on the step
of the open french window
facing each other
your knees held in mine
the blue plates in our laps
the strawberries glistening
in the hot sunlight
we dipped them in sugar
looking at each other
not hurrying the feast
for one to come
the empty plates
laid on the stone together
with the two forks crossed
and I bent towards you
sweet in that air
in my arms
abandoned like a child

from your eager mouth
the taste of strawberries
in my memory
lean back again
let me love you

let the sun beat
on our forgetfulness
one hour of all
the heat intense
and summer lightning
on the Kilpatrick hills

let the storm wash the plates

Moonlit Apples

JOHN DRINKWATER

At the top of the house the apples are laid in rows,
And the skylight lets the moonlight in, and those
Apples are deep-sea apples of green. There goes
A cloud on the moon in the autumn night.

A mouse in the wainscot scratches, and scratches, and then
There is no sound at the top of the house of men
Or mice; and the cloud is blown, and the moon again
Dapples the apples with deep-sea light.

They are lying in rows there, under the gloomy beams;
On the sagging floor; they gather the silver streams
Out of the moon, those moonlit apples of dreams,
And quiet is the steep stair under.

In the corridors under there is nothing but sleep.
And stiller than ever on orchard boughs they keep
Tryst with the moon, and deep is the silence, deep
On moon-washed apples of wonder.

Just Once

CHRIS KINSEY

Dad took me out to the field.

We tunnelled through uncut hay
rolled dens with many rooms.
Cuckoo spit clung to the walls.

When we lay still and watched the sky
he said: *This is where we're coming to live.*

Years after we moved,
I searched for that meadow,

that sky.

Blackberry-Picking

for Philip Hobsbaum

SEAMUS HEANEY

Late August, given heavy rain and sun
For a full week, the blackberries would ripen.
At first, just one, a glossy purple clot
Among others, red, green, hard as a knot.
You ate that first one and its flesh was sweet
Like thickened wine: summer's blood was in it
Leaving stains upon the tongue and lust for
Picking. Then red ones inked up and that hunger
Sent us out with milk cans, pea tins, jam-pots
Where briars scratched and wet grass bleached our boots.
Round hayfields, cornfields and potato-drills
We trekked and picked until the cans were full,
Until the tinkling bottom had been covered
With green ones, and on top big dark blobs burned
Like a plate of eyes. Our hands were peppered
With thorn pricks, our palms sticky as Bluebeard's.

We hoarded the fresh berries in the byre.
But when the bath was filled we found a fur,
A rat-grey fungus, glutting on our cache.

The juice was stinking too. Once off the bush
The fruit fermented, the sweet flesh would turn sour.
I always felt like crying. It wasn't fair
That all the lovely canfuls smelt of rot.
Each year I hoped they'd keep, knew they would not.

Death stands above me

WALTER SAVAGE LANDOR

Death stands above me, whispering low
I know not what into my ear;
Of his strange language all I know
Is, there is not a word of fear.

Just off the A5, West of Llangollen

JONATHAN DAVIDSON

To swing the gate shut and latch it,
And begin to walk up the track
Along the *cwm*, is almost like love.

The stream tilts past you, clattering
The air with the sad gravity
Of tumbling water, a grey light.

The mud gives way to bare rock, splintered
By ancient pressure, pushed from below:
The life that you have lived, the lies told.

The cottage stands ready; slow, heavy slate
Takes your weight, a small desk,
An old chair, outside leaves and hills.

And in the frail, un-leaven Welsh silence
You are pulled back into yourself,
Before the fall, the boy, lost, alone.

Waiting for the Bus

MEG COX

Perhaps my dogs,

that sit at the gate
every morning and bark

will live again
some years from now
in a poem by one of those children
who this morning waits
opposite my field gate
for the school bus,

bare legged in the rain.

Endymion, Book I [extract]

JOHN KEATS

A thing of beauty is a joy for ever:
Its loveliness increases; it will never
Pass into nothingness; but still will keep
A bower quiet for us, and a sleep
Full of sweet dreams, and health, and quiet breathing.
Therefore, on every morrow, are we wreathing
A flowery band to bind us to the earth,
Spite of despondence, of the inhuman dearth
Of noble natures, of the gloomy days,
Of all the unhealthy and o'er-darkened ways
Made for our searching: yes, in spite of all,
Some shape of beauty moves away the pall
From our dark spirits. Such the sun, the moon,
Trees old and young, sprouting a shady boon
For simple sheep; and such are daffodils
With the green world they live in.

The Malvern Hills

for Liz Flanagan

BETHANY RIVERS

The Malvern Hills
are in bloom again –
with roses that wouldn't grow
at the old house
in Llansantffraid – this must prove
how despite the grief
over rotting leeks, damp firewood,
wingless car and frost bitten strawberries,
that life is exactly
how it's supposed to be,
as I grow into my new heart
cracks, re-silver them
and call it home.

Going Home

for my grandmother, Theresa Frank

SHERYL ST. GERMAIN

Some slow evenings when the light hangs late and
    stubborn in the sky,
gives itself up to darkness slowly and deliberately, slow
    cloud after slow cloud,
slowness enters me like something familiar,
and it feels like going home.

It's all there in the disappearing light:
all the evenings of slow sky and slow loving, slow boats
    on sluggish bayous;
the thick-middled trees with the slow-sounding names –
    oak, mimosa, pecan, magnolia;
the slow tree sap that sticks in your hair when you lie
    with the trees;
and the maple syrup and pancakes and grits, the butter
    melting
slowly into and down the sides like sweat between
    breasts of sloe-eyed strippers;
and the slow-throated blues that floats over the city
    like fog;

and the weeping, the willows, the cut onions, the cayenne,
the slow-cooking beans with marrow-thick gravy;
and all the mint juleps drunk so slowly on all the slow
southern porches,
the bourbon and sugar and mint going down warm and
brown, syrup and slow;
and all the ice cubes melting in all the iced teas,
all the slow-faced people sitting in all the slowly rocking
rockers;
and the crabs and the shrimp and crawfish, the hard shells
slowly and deliberately and lovingly removed, the
delicate flesh
slowly sucked out of heads and legs and tails;
and the slow lips that eat and drink and love and speak
that slow luxurious language, savoring each word like a
long-missed lover;
and the slow-moving nuns, the black habits dragging the
swollen ground;
and the slow river that cradles it all, and the chicory coffee
that cuts through it all, slow-boiled and black as dirt;
and the slow dreams and the slow-healing wounds and
the slow smoke of it all
slipping out, ballooning into the sky – slow, deliberate,
and magnificent.

Sudden Light

DANTE GABRIEL ROSSETTI

I have been here before,
But when or how I cannot tell:
I know the grass beyond the door,
The sweet keen smell,
The sighing sound, the lights around the shore.

You have been mine before, –
How long ago I may not know:
But just when at that swallow's soar
Your neck turn'd so,
Some veil did fall, – I knew it all of yore.

Has this been thus before?
And shall not thus time's eddying flight
Still with our lives our love restore
In death's despite,
And day and night yield one delight once more?

Old Man

EDWARD THOMAS

Old Man, or Lad's-love, – in the name there's nothing
To one that knows not Lad's-love, or Old Man,
The hoar-green feathery herb, almost a tree,
Growing with rosemary and lavender.
Even to one that knows it well, the names
Half decorate, half perplex, the thing it is:
At least, what that is clings not to the names
In spite of time. And yet I like the names.

The herb itself I like not, but for certain
I love it, as some day the child will love it
Who plucks a feather from the door-side bush
Whenever she goes in or out of the house.
Often she waits there, snipping the tips and shrivelling
The shreds at last on to the path, perhaps
Thinking, perhaps of nothing, till she sniffs
Her fingers and runs off. The bush is still
But half as tall as she, though it is as old;
So well she clips it. Not a word she says;
And I can only wonder how much hereafter
She will remember, with that bitter scent,

Of garden rows, and ancient damson-trees
Topping a hedge, a bent path to a door,
A low thick bush beside the door, and me
Forbidding her to pick.

As for myself,
Where first I met the bitter scent is lost.
I, too, often shrivel the grey shreds,
Sniff them and think and sniff again and try
Once more to think what it is I am remembering,
Always in vain. I cannot like the scent,
Yet I would rather give up others more sweet,
With no meaning, than this bitter one.

I have mislaid the key. I sniff the spray
And think of nothing; I see and I hear nothing;
Yet seem, too, to be listening, lying in wait
For what I should, yet never can, remember:
No garden appears, no path, no hoar-green bush
Of Lad's-love, or Old Man, no child beside,
Neither father nor mother, nor any playmate;
Only an avenue, dark, nameless, without end.

Dover Beach [extract]

MATTHEW ARNOLD

The sea is calm tonight.
The tide is full, the moon lies fair
Upon the straits; on the French coast the light
Gleams and is gone; the cliffs of England stand,
Glimmering and vast, out in the tranquil bay.
Come to the window, sweet is the night-air!
Only, from the long line of spray
Where the sea meets the moon-blanched land,
Listen! you hear the grating roar
Of pebbles which the waves draw back, and fling,
At their return, up the high strand,
Begin, and cease, and then again begin,
With tremulous cadence slow, and bring
The eternal note of sadness in.

An upper chamber in a darkened house

FREDERICK GODDARD TUCKERMAN

An upper chamber in a darkened house,
Where, ere his footsteps reached ripe manhood's brink,
Terror and anguish were his cup to drink;
I cannot rid the thought, nor hold it close
But dimly dream upon that man alone:
Now though the autumn clouds most softly pass,
The cricket chides beneath the doorstep stone,
And greener than the season grows the grass.
Nor can I drop my lids, nor shade my brows,
But there he stands beside the lifted sash;
And with a swooning of the heart, I think
Where the black shingles slope to meet the boughs,
And, shattered on the roof like smallest snows,
The tiny petals of the mountain-ash.

You are old, Father William

LEWIS CARROLL

'You are old, Father William,' the young man said,
'And your hair has become very white;
And yet you incessantly stand on your head –
Do you think, at your age, it is right?'

'In my youth,' Father William replied to his son,
'I feared it might injure the brain;
But, now that I'm perfectly sure I have none,
Why, I do it again and again.'

'You are old,' said the youth, 'as I mentioned before,
And have grown most uncommonly fat;
Yet you turned a back-somersault in at the door –
Pray, what is the reason of that?'

'In my youth,' said the sage, as he shook his grey locks,
'I kept all my limbs very supple
By the use of this ointment – one shilling the box –
Allow me to sell you a couple?'

'You are old,' said the youth, 'and your jaws are too weak
For anything tougher than suet;
Yet you finished the goose, with the bones and the beak –
Pray, how did you manage to do it?'

'In my youth,' said his father, 'I took to the law,
And argued each case with my wife;
And the muscular strength, which it gave to my jaw,
Has lasted the rest of my life.'

'You are old,' said the youth, 'one would hardly suppose
That your eye was as steady as ever;
Yet you balanced an eel on the end of your nose –
What made you so awfully clever?'

'I have answered three questions, and that is enough,'
Said his father; 'don't give yourself airs!
Do you think I can listen all day to such stuff?
Be off, or I'll kick you downstairs!'

Rain

EDWARD THOMAS

Rain, midnight rain, nothing but the wild rain
On this bleak hut, and solitude, and me
Remembering again that I shall die
And neither hear the rain nor give it thanks
For washing me cleaner than I have been
Since I was born into this solitude.
Blessed are the dead that the rain rains upon:
But here I pray that none whom once I loved
Is dying to-night or lying still awake
Solitary, listening to the rain,
Either in pain or thus in sympathy
Helpless among the living and the dead,
Like a cold water among broken reeds,
Myriads of broken reeds all still and stiff,
Like me who have no love which this wild rain
Has not dissolved except the love of death,
If love it be towards what is perfect and
Cannot, the tempest tells me, disappoint.

Life

HENRY VAN DYKE

Let me but live my life from year to year,
With forward face and unreluctant soul;
Not hurrying to, nor turning from the goal;
Not mourning for the things that disappear
In the dim past, nor holding back in fear
From what the future veils; but with a whole
And happy heart, that pays its toll
To Youth and Age, and travels on with cheer.

So let the way wind up the hill or down,
O'er rough or smooth, the journey will be joy:
Still seeking what I sought when but a boy,
New friendship, high adventure, and a crown,
My heart will keep the courage of the quest,
And hope the road's last turn will be the best.

Live Broadcast

JONATHAN DAVIDSON

Too late to go out and nowhere to go
anyway, I content myself with this
celestial but dis-contenting music,

some stuff by J S Bach which they enjoy
in London very well. Your message says
you're sitting down to listen to it too,

while busying yourself with things that must
be done or looking briefly at the last
high clouds. Although we are alone the Gods

of digital transmission have ensured
the sound they give to you they give to me.
Now all that is between us is the music,

that breaks into the orbit of our hearts
– no, really; so I believe – and holds us
like asteroids on such trajectories

decided by the pull of time and place,

until the final notes have crossed the sky,
until the final light-show of applause,

at which we are let go into the dark.

What are heavy?
CHRISTINA ROSSETTI

What are heavy? Sea-sand and sorrow:
What are brief? To-day and to-morrow:
What are frail? Spring blossoms and youth:
What are deep? The ocean and truth.

The Word
MYRA SCHNEIDER

I awaken, muddled, to slovenly bedclothes,
the blur-grey of drizzle. Back and legs are sluggish.

Difficult to pretend I'm not getting old –
yesterday's visitor rubbed it in as she smiled

at our wallpaper: *lovely sixties – pity it's out of date.*
Unbirthday weather but I set out with self
and presents swaddled in layers of plastic.
Serious rain at Finsbury Park so I stick

my head into the dim of the minicab office
instead of trudging to the flock of dozing buses.
The spectacled woman behind the desk is dipping
bread into a carton of winter vegetable soup

in spite of the no-eating notice pinned to the wall.
Five minutes, have a rest. Her comfortable
black face distracts me from the weeping windows.
How old are you? she asks out of the blue.

No way to wriggle out of revealing the truth.
A pause. *You don't look it – you're gorgeous.*
It's not true but I sit up straight and face tingling,
stuff the word in my pocket – it goes on singing!

Sea-Fever

JOHN MASEFIELD

I must go down to the seas again, to the lonely sea and
the sky,
And all I ask is a tall ship and a star to steer her by;
And the wheel's kick and the wind's song and the white
sail's shaking,
And a grey mist on the sea's face, and a grey dawn
breaking.

I must go down to the seas again, for the call of the
running tide
Is a wild call and a clear call that may not be denied;
And all I ask is a windy day with the white clouds flying,
And the flung spray and the blown spume, and the sea-
gulls crying.

I must go down to the seas again, to the vagrant gypsy life,
To the gull's way and the whale's way where the wind's
like a whetted knife;
And all I ask is a merry yarn from a laughing fellow-rover,
And quiet sleep and a sweet dream when the long trick's
over.

Where Go the Boats?

ROBERT LOUIS STEVENSON

Dark brown is the river,
    Golden is the sand.
It flows along for ever,
    With trees on either hand.

Green leaves a-floating,
    Castles of the foam,
Boats of mine a-boating –
    Where will all come home?

On goes the river
    And out past the mill,
Away down the valley,
    Away down the hill.

Away down the river,
    A hundred miles or more,
Other little children
    Shall bring my boats ashore.

For the Anniversary of My Death

W. S. MERWIN

Every year without knowing it I have passed the day
When the last fires will wave to me
And the silence will set out
Tireless traveler
Like the beam of a lightless star

Then I will no longer
Find myself in life as in a strange garment
Surprised at the earth
And the love of one woman
And the shamelessness of men
As today writing after three days of rain
Hearing the wren sing and the falling cease
And bowing not knowing to what

Eden Rock

CHARLES CAUSLEY

They are waiting for me somewhere beyond Eden Rock:
My father, twenty-five, in the same suit
Of Genuine Irish Tweed, his terrier Jack
Still two years old and trembling at his feet.

My mother, twenty-three, in a sprigged dress
Drawn at the waist, ribbon in her straw hat,
Has spread the stiff white cloth over the grass.
Her hair, the colour of wheat, takes on the light.

She pours tea from a Thermos, the milk straight
From an old H.P. sauce-bottle, a screw
Of paper for a cork; slowly sets out
The same three plates, the tin cups painted blue.

The sky whitens as if lit by three suns.
My mother shades her eyes and looks my way
Over the drifted stream. My father spins
A stone along the water. Leisurely,
They beckon to me from the other bank.

I hear them call, 'See where the stream-path is!
Crossing is not as hard as you might think.'

I had not thought that it would be like this.

O You Angels, Who Guard the People

JEAN ATKIN

The house breathed like a sleeper,
just audible in doorways. Its walls exhaled
a sifting into silence.
And all the centuries hanging there
like soot in the chimney.
When I stood under it and looked up
it was a wide door to the stars
and the cold fell down on us each December.

I used to put my hands on the walls,
which were cool and chalky and bulbous.
I was skin to skin with the house
and skin to skin with the babies.

I used to listen with my fingers, flatten my palms,
cajole deep memories out of walls:
calls, cries and prayers soaked into stone.
The ghosts walking, lifting latches.

We played Hildegard von Bingen to the house
O vosangeli, qui custoditispopulos –
sounds so old even this house was unquarried:
each silver note snagged
on iron window catches.
And since we've left, our voices,
and our children's, must be suspended there
in falling lime dust.

Requiem

ROBERT LOUIS STEVENSON

Under the wide and starry sky
　　Dig the grave and let me lie.
Glad did I live and gladly die,
　　And I laid me down with a will.

This be the verse you grave for me;
　　'Here he lies where he longed to be,
Home is the sailor, home from sea,
　　And the hunter home from the hill.'

FIELD GUIDE

Tony Hoagland's poem 'Field Guide' introduces us in the most beautifully simple way to the pleasure of being out in the natural world, of what it is to be connected to the earth and what it can give back to us.

I love the playfulness and earthiness of David Morley's poem 'The Ditch,' which imagines the eighteenth-century poet John Clare 'down by the ditch, where he writes,' alongside two glorious poems by Clare himself.

Field Guide

TONY HOAGLAND

Once, in the cool blue middle of a lake,
up to my neck in that most precious element of all,

I found a pale-gray, curled-upwards pigeon feather
floating on the tension of the water

at the very instant when a dragonfly,
like a blue-green iridescent bobby pin,

hovered over it, then lit, and rested.
That's all.

I mention this in the same way
that I fold the corner of a page

in certain library books,
so that the reader will know

where to look for the good parts.

The Tables Turned

WILLIAM WORDSWORTH

Up! up! my Friend, and quit your books;
Or surely you'll grow double:
Up! up! my Friend, and clear your looks;
Why all this toil and trouble?

The sun above the mountain's head,
A freshening lustre mellow
Through all the long green fields has spread,
His first sweet evening yellow.

Books! 'tis a dull and endless strife:
Come, hear the woodland linnet,
How sweet his music! on my life,
There's more of wisdom in it.

And hark! how blithe the throstle sings!
He, too, is no mean preacher:
Come forth into the light of things,
Let Nature be your teacher.

She has a world of ready wealth,
Our minds and hearts to bless –
Spontaneous wisdom breathed by health,
Truth breathed by cheerfulness.

One impulse from a vernal wood
May teach you more of man,
Of moral evil and of good,
Than all the sages can.

Sweet is the lore which Nature brings;
Our meddling intellect
Mis-shapes the beauteous forms of things:–
We murder to dissect.

Enough of Science and of Art;
Close up those barren leaves;
Come forth, and bring with you a heart
That watches and receives.

To a Skylark [extract]

PERCY BYSSHE SHELLEY

Hail to thee, blithe Spirit!
Bird thou never wert,
That from Heaven, or near it,
Pourest thy full heart
In profuse strains of unpremeditated art.

Higher still and higher
From the earth thou springest
Like a cloud of fire;
The blue deep thou wingest,
And singing still dost soar, and soaring ever singest.

In the golden lightning
Of the sunken sun,
O'er which clouds are bright'ning,
Thou dost float and run;
Like an unbodied joy whose race is just begun.

The pale purple even
Melts around thy flight;
Like a star of Heaven,

In the broad day-light
Thou art unseen, but yet I hear thy shrill delight,

Keen as are the arrows
Of that silver sphere,
Whose intense lamp narrows
In the white dawn clear
Until we hardly see, we feel that it is there.

I So Liked Spring

CHARLOTTE MEW

I so liked Spring last year
Because you were here; –
The thrushes too –
Because it was these you so liked to hear –
I so liked you.

This year's a different thing, –
I'll not think of you.
But I'll like the Spring because it is simply spring
As the thrushes do

Emmonsail's Heath in Winter

JOHN CLARE

I love to see the old heath's withered brake
Mingle its crimpled leaves with furze and ling,
While the old heron from the lonely lake
Starts slow and flaps its melancholy wing,
An oddling crow in idle motion swing
On the half-rotten ash-tree's topmost twig,
Beside whose trunk the gypsy makes his bed.
Up flies the bouncing woodcock from the brig
Where a black quagmire quakes beneath the tread;
The fieldfares chatter in the whistling thorn
And for the haw round fields and closen rove,
And coy bumbarrels, twenty in a drove,
Flit down the hedgerows in the frozen plain
And hang on little twigs and start again.

The Ditch

DAVID MORLEY

I used to drop down behind a hedge bush or dyke and
write down my things upon the crown of my hat.

As John Clare rises from the ditch where he writes,
frogs bob up through duckweed and roll their eyelids,
The poet's coat and hat, they thought, *were rainclouds.*
The scribbling pen and riffling paper: they were the rain.
The cloud and rain have moved like lovers out of sight.
Woodlice wake under bark. Nests nudge from within.
Buds are easter-hedged with eggs. A world unwinds
unwinding a world: hedges are easter-egged with buds;
woodlice wake under nests; bark nudges from within;
the lovers and rain move like clouds out of sight;
a scribbling paper and riffling rain: they are the pen;
a thought's hat and coat and rain-cloud: they are the poets;
frogs roll up through duckweed and bob their eyelids.
And John Clare settles down by the ditch, where he writes.

To the Fox Fern
JOHN CLARE

Haunter of woods, lone wilds and solitudes
Where none but feet of birds and things as wild
Doth print a foot track near, where summer's light
Buried in boughs forgets its glare and round thy crimped
    leaves
Feints in a quiet dimness fit for musings
And melancholy moods, with here and there
A golden thread of sunshine stealing through
The evening shadowy leaves that seem to creep
Like leisure in the shade.

Birds at Winter Nightfall
THOMAS HARDY

Around the house the flakes fly faster,
And all the berries now are gone
From holly and cotoneaster
Around the house. The flakes fly! – faster

Shutting indoors that crumb-outcaster
We used to see upon the lawn
Around the house. The flakes fly faster,
And all the berries now are gone!

The Twist in the River

KATHERINE PIERPOINT

At the clear, beer-coloured and bubbleshot twist in the
    river –
Every stone a speckled egg spawned in that deep lap,
Every pockmarked, pitted pebble a planet, blindly seeing
    through its own evolution –
The shallows, and the tall air, are filled with sound and
    light.
This part of the river expects to be seen, for it has drawn
    you there,
And the trees, selfless, introduce the sky into your love
    for the water.
If this place were a person, it would be making up a
    paper hat while humming –

Entirely self-contained, absorbed yet radiant –
A family moment, appearing normal until years later in
    retrospect,
When its depth are fully felt, beyond blunt experience.

Underwater, the light thickens slightly but never sets
And the river runs through its own fingers.

The Wild Swans at Coole

WILLIAM BUTLER YEATS

The trees are in their autumn beauty,
The woodland paths are dry,
Under the October twilight the water
Mirrors a still sky;
Upon the brimming water among the stones
Are nine-and-fifty swans.

The nineteenth autumn has come upon me
Since I first made my count;
I saw, before I had well finished,

All suddenly mount
And scatter wheeling in great broken rings
Upon their clamorous wings.

I have looked upon those brilliant creatures,
And now my heart is sore.
All's changed since I, hearing at twilight,
The first time on this shore,
The bell-beat of their wings above my head,
Trod with a lighter tread.

Unwearied still, lover by lover,
They paddle in the cold
Companionable streams or climb the air;
Their hearts have not grown old;
Passion or conquest, wander where they will,
Attend upon them still.

But now they drift on the still water,
Mysterious, beautiful;
Among what rushes will they build,
By what lake's edge or pool
Delight men's eyes when I awake some day
To find they have flown away?

Wuthering Heights

SYLVIA PLATH

The horizons ring me like faggots,
Tilted and disparate, and always unstable.
Touched by a match, they might warm me,
And their fine lines singe
The air to orange
Before the distances they pin evaporate,
Weighting the pale sky with a soldier color.
But they only dissolve and dissolve
Like a series of promises, as I step forward.

There is no life higher than the grasstops
Or the hearts of sheep, and the wind
Pours by like destiny, bending
Everything in one direction.
I can feel it trying
To funnel my heat away.
If I pay the roots of the heather
Too close attention, they will invite me
To whiten my bones among them.

The sheep know where they are,
Browsing in their dirty wool-clouds,
Grey as the weather.
The black slots of their pupils take me in.
It is like being mailed into space,
A thin, silly message.
They stand about in grandmotherly disguise,
All wig curls and yellow teeth
And hard, marbly baas.

I come to wheel ruts, and water
Limpid as the solitudes
That flee through my fingers.
Hollow doorsteps go from grass to grass;
Lintel and sill have unhinged themselves.
Of people the air only
Remembers a few odd syllables.
It rehearses them moaningly:
Black stone, black stone.

The sky leans on me, me, the one upright
Among the horizontals.
The grass is beating its head distractedly.
It is too delicate

For a life in such company;
Darkness terrifies it.
Now, in valleys narrow
And black as purses, the house lights
Gleam like small change.

Only some spires

EMILY BRONTË

Only some spires of bright green grass
Transparently in sunshine quivering.

The spaces where breath goes

The everyday world can also be complicated
– work is stressful, our futures uncertain
and there can sometimes seem so much
injustice. There is a growing awareness of
the need to counter the anxiety that is an
understandable consequence. Many people
turn to deeper and older wisdoms, ones
that speak of mindfulness, meditation and

help us to achieve this
and show us where it

ROSE O¹²
MOISTURE DEFENCE
OIL

HUILE ROSE O¹²
BOUCLIER HYDRATANT

2ml℮/0.07fl.oz

The Small Window

R. S. THOMAS

In Wales there are jewels
To gather, but with the eye
Only. A hill lights up
Suddenly; a field trembles
With colour and goes out
In its turn; in one day
You can witness the extent
Of the spectrum and grow rich
With looking. Have a care;
The wealth is for the few
And chosen. Those who crowd
A small window dirty it
With their breathing, though sublime
And inexhaustible the view.

Green

D. H. LAWRENCE

The dawn was apple-green,
The sky was green wine held up in the sun,
The moon was a golden petal between.

She opened her eyes, and green
They shone, clear like flowers undone
For the first time, now for the first time seen.

How Do I Become the Very Ground?

JANE BURN

I have this need for fields.
For the way they sink me, pull me footwards –
root yourself, they offer.
This swallowing of my boots, lodged
in clunching cheeks – they chew
a welcome around my feet. Spring is coming.
I open my dirty coat

like a tree-bud, unzipping canvas scales,
showing humps of breast
to the front of the sun. I am a furly Comfrey bloom.
I wish to wear a crown
of bumble bees upon my head, to offer
their mouths my honey hair.
Be rested on our sponge of moss. The horses, bedded
down in splints of light
have learned this – groan their utter pleasure
in this heated fur,
ask no more of the afternoon.

Theory of Light

JOAN FLEMING

Andy goes craving all over the beach
with her red grip and her red grapple.

A red apple after dark isn't red,
it's a black apple.

She says she'll black up if she doesn't have salt.
She finds a sea urchin full of holes.

What's a blue sea after dark?
Are these the spaces where breath goes?

I find a gorgeous gold-yellow branch,
a colour, a describable friend.

We carry our findings, our branches
and urchins, from end to end.

The blue and red and yellow everywhere
is our theory of colour, of light.

Young salt-footed fools, you know there are no ends,
only ends in sight.

And in the 51st Year of That Century, While My Brother Cried in the Trench, While My Enemy Glared from the Cave

HYAM PLUTZIK

This star is only an augury of the morning,
Gift-bearer of another day.

A wind has brought the musk of thirty fields,
Each like a coin of silver under that sky.

Precious, the soundless breathing of wife and children
In a house on a field lit by the morning star.

Autumn

T. E. HULME

A touch of cold in the Autumn night –
I walked abroad,
And saw the ruddy moon lean over a hedge
Like a red-faced farmer.
I did not stop to speak, but nodded,

And round about were the wistful stars
With white faces like town children.

Chorus

NIGEL McLOUGHLIN

A thousand webs barely contain the green thrum
of the hedge and the night-drop dregs of silver
burst in the mouth; reek like zest. The eye irradiates
with a clamour of birds blackening into horizon.
Colour begins a slow thunder across the sky, multiplies
and changes; sings in bird-throat to the beat of wings.
The air hives with birth, vibrates out of shadow.
Everything burns, everything rings, including me.

The great bell of the world vibrates and I am drunk
with winter-shine. The concrete blazes. The red tang
of seven o'clock and the vein-belt of walking brazen
to the frost leaps through me. An hour before petrol-stink
and the shrink of people diminishing into a rush, here
in the open-throated song of morning, I am in the clear.

Under Milk Wood [extract]

DYLAN THOMAS

The lust and lilt and lather and emerald green breeze
and crackle of the bird-praise and body of Spring with its
breasts full of rivering May-milk …

The sunny slow lulling afternoon yawns and moons
through the dozy town. The sea lolls, laps and idles
in, with fishes sleeping in its lap. The meadows still as
Sunday, the shut-eye tasselled bulls, the goat-and-daisy
dingles, nap happy and lazy. The dumb duck-ponds
snooze. Clouds sag and pillow on Llaregyb Hill. Pigs
grunt in a wet wallow-bath, and smile as they snort and
dream. They dream of the acorned swill of the world,
the rooting for pig-fruit, the bag-pipe dugs' of the mother
sow, the squeal and snuffle of yesses of the women pigs
in rut. They mud-bask and snout in the pig-loving sun;
their tails curl; they rollick and slobber and snore to
deep, smug, after-swill sleep.

High Summer

EBENEZER JONES

I never wholly feel that summer is high,
However green the grass, or loud the birds,
However movelessly eye-winking herds
Stand in field ponds, or under large trees lie,
Till I do climb all cultured pastures by,
That hedged by hedgerows studiously fretted trim,
Smile like a lady's face with lace laced prim,
And on some moor or hill that seeks the sky
Lonely and nakedly, – utterly lie down,
And feel the sunshine throbbing on body and limb,
My drowsy brain in pleasant drunkenness swim,
Each rising thought sink back, and dreamily drown,
Smiles creep o'er my face, and smother my lips, and cloy,
Each muscle sink to itself, and separately enjoy.

Grace

ESTHER MORGAN

You've been living for this for weeks
without knowing it:

the moment the house empties like a city in August
so completely
it forgets you exist.

Light withdraws slowly
is almost gone before you notice.

In the stillness, everything becomes itself:
the circle of white plates on the kitchen table
the serious chairs that attend them

even the roses on the papered walls
seem to open a little wider.

It looks simple: the glass vase holding
whatever is offered –
cut flowers, or the thought of them –

simple, though not easy
this waiting without hunger in the near dark
for what you may be about to receive.

Arrival

R. S. THOMAS

Not conscious
that you have been seeking
suddenly
you come upon it

the village in the Welsh hills
dust free
with no road out
but the one you came in by.

A bird chimes
from a green tree
the hour that is no hour
you know. The river dawdles

to hold a mirror for you
where you may see yourself
as you are, a traveller
with the moon's halo
above him, whom has arrived
after long journeying where he
began, catching this
one truth by surprise
that there is everything to look forward to.

The Last Poem

JAMES SHEARD

The last poem was not wrought.
It was not inlaid. It was unveined.

It was not a mechanism, skeletal
or industrial. It was not set ticking

by the moving fingers of a craftsman
or soothed upwards into blossom.

And because it was never open,
the last poem did not click shut

with a pleasing sound, like a box
with a perfect hinge and a perfect catch.

It held no jewels.

The last poem was not luminous.
It did not vibrate. It evoked

not very much at all.

It sat fat and leaden in the hand, like that.
It curled the holder's fingers around it,

just so.

ACKNOWLEDGEMENTS

I'd like to thank everyone at Michael O'Mara Books for giving me this second opportunity to be self-indulgent in my selection of poems. I'd particularly like to thank George Maudsley for his unfailing patience, support and gentle nagging.

Thank you so much to the following poets for their friendship and their generosity with their poems, which have brought this anthology to life: Jean Atkin, Carole Bromley, Jane Burn, Thirza Clout, Meg Cox, Jonathan Davidson, Angela France, Robert Harper, Steve Harrison, Lesley Ingram, Chris Kinsey, Char March, Lisa Oliver, Jeff Phelps, Wendy Pratt, Angela Readman, Maggie Mackay, Bethany Rivers, Jaqueline Saphra, Myra Schneider, James Sheard and Angela Topping. I am so very grateful.

And love and thanks as always to Jim for his love and confidence in me.

Recommended reading

Albery, Nicholas (Ed.), *Poem for the Day*, 1994 (Chatto & Windus)

Astley, Neil (Ed.), *Being Alive*, 2004 (Bloodaxe)

Astley, Neil (Ed.), *Being Human*, 2011 (Bloodaxe)

Astley, Neil (Ed.), *Staying Alive*, 2002 (Bloodaxe)

Astley, Neil & Robertson-Pearce, Pamela (Ed.), *Soul Food: Nourishing Poems for Starved Minds*, 2007 (Bloodaxe)

Barber, Laura, *Poems for Life*, 2007 (Penguin Classics)

Goodwin, Daisy (Ed.), *100 Poems to See You Through*, 2014 (Ebury)

CREDITS

The author and publisher are grateful to the following for permission to use material that is in copyright:

John Agard: 'Coffee in Heaven' from *Alternative Anthem: Selected Poems* (Bloodaxe Books, 2009) reproduced with the permission of Bloodaxe Books.

Jean Atkin: 'O You Angels, Who Guard the People' from *Not Lost Since Last Time* by Jean Atkin, published by Oversteps Books Ltd., 2013.

Eavan Boland: 'Quarantine' from *New Collected Poems* (Carcanet Press, 2005) reproduced with the permission of Carcanet Press Limited.

Alison Brackenbury: 'Friday Afternoon' from *Skies* (Carcanet Press, 2016) reproduced with the permission of Carcanet Press Limited.

Charles Causley: 'Eden Rock' from *Collected Poems 1951–2000* (Macmillan) reproduced with the permission of David Higham Associates Limited.

Thirza Clout: 'My Mother's Arts' from *The Bone Seeker* (Mark Time Books UK, 2016).

Meg Cox: 'Summer Holidays', 'Today's Headlines' and 'Waiting for the Bus' from *Looking Over My Shoulder at Sodom* published by Hen Run, an imprint of Grey Hen Press.

Char March: 'Washing My Mother's Hair' from *The Thousand Natural Shocks* (Indigo Dreams Publishing), reproduced with the kind permission of the author and publisher.

John Masefield: 'Sea-Fever' reproduced with the permission of The Society of Authors as the Literary Representative of the Estate of John Masefield.

Roger McGough: 'Summer with Monika' reproduced with the permission of Peters, Fraser & Dunlop.

Michelle McGrane: 'Thirteen Ways with Figs' from *The Suitable Girl* reproduced with the kind permission of the author and Pindrop Press.

Nigel McLoughlin: 'Chorus' from *Chora: New and Selected Poems* (Templar Poetry, 2009) reproduced with the kind permission of the author.

W. S. Merwin: 'For the Anniversary of My Death' from *Selected Poems* (Bloodaxe Books, 2007) reproduced with the permission of Bloodaxe Books.

Edwin Morgan: 'Strawberries' from *The Second Life* (Edinburgh University Press, 1968) and later *New Selected Poems* (Carcanet Press, 2000), reproduced with the permission of Carcanet Press Limited.

Esther Morgan: 'Grace' (Bloodaxe Books, 2011) reproduced with the permission of Bloodaxe Books.

INDEX OF POETS

Agard, John 46
Arnold, Matthew 130
Atkin, Jean 143
Barrett Browning, Elizabeth 88
Boland, Eavan 14
Brackenbury, Alison 38
Bromley, Carole 62
Brontë, Emily 160
Burn, Jane 24, 163
Byron, Lord 48
Campion, Thomas 87
Carroll, Lewis 132
Causley, Charles 142
Clare, John 152, 154
Clout, Thirza 67
Cox, Meg 18, 52, 122
Davidson, Jonathan 26, 121, 136
De la O, Marsha 106
Dickinson, Emily 109
Donne, John 82
Drinkwater, John 117
Dunn, Stephen 58
Douglas, Keith 84
Fleming, Joan 164
France, Angela 89
Gillilan, Pamela 110
Hardy, Thomas 20, 50, 154

Harper, Robert 15
Harrison, Steve 69
Hayden, Robert 68
Heaney, Seamus 99, 119
Herrick, Robert 54
Hikmet, Nazim 33
Hill, Selima 79
Hoagland, Tony 147
Hughes, Ted 73
Hulme, T. E. 166
Ingram, Lesley 66, 104
Jones, Ebenezer 169
Jonson, Ben 97
Kaplisnki, Jaan 75
Keats, John 94, 123
Kenyon, Jane 25
Keyes, Sidney 91, 109
Kinsey, Chris 118
Landor, Walter Savage 120
Lasker-Schuler, Else 80
Lawrence, D. H. 28, 36, 40, 61, 163
Levertov, Denise 53
Mackay, Maggie 105
March, Char 102
Marquis, Don 70
Masefield, John 139
McGough, Roger 85
McGrane, Michelle 41

McLoughlin, Nigel 167
Merwin, W. S. 141
Mew, Charlotte 151
Millay, Edna St Vincent 93
Morgan, Edwin 115
Morgan, Esther 170
Morley, David 153
Mort, Helen 13
Oliver, Lisa 46
Phelps, Jeff 57
Pierpoint, Katherine 155
Plath, Sylvia 98, 158
Plutzik, Hyam 166
Pratt, Wendy 21
Pushkin, Alexander 92
Readman, Angela 112
Rivers, Bethany 124
Rossetti, Christina 137
Rossetti, Dante Gabriel 127
Saphra, Jacqueline 63
Schneider, Myra 137
Shakespeare, William 86, 90
Shapcott, Jo 100
Sheard, James 76, 172
Shelley, Percy Bysshe 150
Southey, Fraser 72
Sprackland, Jean 95
St. Germain, Sheryl 125
Stevenson, Robert Louis 64,
    140, 145
Taylor Coleridge, Samuel 17
Teasdale, Sara 19

Tennyson, Alfred, Lord 23
Thomas, Dylan 49, 168
Thomas, Edward 128, 134
Thomas, R. S. 162, 171
Topping, Angela 107
Tuckerman, Frederick
    Goddard 131
Van Dyke, Henry 135
Whitman, Walt 29, 82
Wickham, Anna 51
Williams, Hugo 65
Williams, William Carlos 32
Wordsworth, William 16,
    148
Yasunaga, Caroline 27
Yeats, William Butler 96, 156
Zagajewski, Adam 12

Index of titles, first lines and notable lines

(**bold** type = titles; plain type = first lines; *italic* type = notable lines. The articles 'the' and 'a(n)' are ignored for sorting purposes)

About the lilting house and happy as the grass was green 49

all I know / Is, there is not a word of fear 120

All Nature seems at work. Slugs leave their lair 17

all the slow-faced people sitting in all the slowly rocking rockers 126

And all I ask is a tall ship and a star to steer her by 139

And all that mighty heart is lying still! 16

And all the berries now are gone 154

And all the centuries hanging there / like soot in the chimney 143

And be, oh be / a sun to me 37

And day and night yield one delight once more? 127

And green and golden I was huntsman and herdsman 49

And hark! how blithe the throstle sings! 148

And honoured among wagons I was prince of the apple towns 49

And Hope without an object cannot live 17

And I fall asleep with the gods, the gods ... 29

And I have watched the women growing old 51

And I laid me down with a will 145

And I should like so much to play, / To have to go to bed by day? 65

And I will see him gather up my life 27

And if those doors to other worlds exist 13

and if we embrace, we will not die 81

And in my heart there stirs a quiet pain 93

and in silence nursed a burning stone 68

And in the 51st Year of That Century ... 166

And now good-morrow to our waking souls 83

And summer's lease hath all too short a date 90

And the hunter home from the hill 145

and the sun is a flame-white disc 32

and 300 circus fleas dead of cold 18

And up we rose, and on the spur we went 23

And we still drink from your silver cup 110

Andy goes craving all over the beach 164

April again, and it's a year again 110

April morning, rain first thing 73

Around the house the flakes fly faster 154

Arrival 171–2

As John Clare rises from the ditch where he writes 153

As what he loves may never like too much 97

ask no more of the afternoon 164

At midnight in the alley 69

At the clear, beer-coloured and bubbleshot twist in the river 155

At the top of the house the apples are laid in rows 117
At twilight she is still sitting with the book in her hand 104
Auntie stands by the kettle, looking at the kettle 100–1
Autumn 166–7

Baby Running Barefoot 61–2
Because it was these you so liked to hear 151
Bed in Summer 64–5
Beehive proppers backcomb teasers 63
Before the fall, the boy, lost, alone 121
The bell-beat of their wings above my head 157
Bird thou never wert 150
Birds at Winter Nightfall 154–5
Blackberry-Picking 119
Blessed are the dead that the rain rains upon 134
Bloom, O ye amaranths! bloom for whom ye may 17
body of Spring with its breasts full of rivering May-milk 168
The bustle in a house 110
The bustle in a house 110
But I'll like the Spring because it is simply spring 151

Canoe 84
A careless shoe-string, in whose tie / I see a wild civility 55
Cargo Cult 74–5
The clear vowels rise like balloons 99
Chorus 167
Coffee in Heaven 46
Cold comforts set between us, things to share 99
Colour begins a slow thunder across the sky 167
Come to the window, sweet is the night-air! 130
Coming home with the silent and dark-cheek'd bush-boy 31
Composed Upon Westminster Bridge, September 3, 1802 16
The cricket chides beneath the doorstep stone 131
The cwtch in my arms 67

Dad took me out to the field 118
Danse Russe 32
Dapples the apples with deep-sea light 117
Dark brown is the river 140
The Darkling Thrush 20–1
The dawn was apple-green 163
a day when children played and did not fall 38
Death stands above me 120
Death stands above me, whispering low 120
Delight in Disorder 54–5
Difficult to pretend I'm not getting old 138
Dirty Bird 24
The Ditch 153
The Doubtful Season 92–3
The doubtful season of the brain's black weather 92
Dover Beach [extract] 130

Earth has not anything to show more fair: 16
Eden Rock 142–3
Elegy 110–11
Emmonsail's Heath in Winter 152
Endymion, Book I [extract] 123
The evening advances, then withdraws again 65
The evening shadowy leaves that seem to creep / Like leisure in the shade 154
Every year without knowing it I have passed the day 141

Far from the sea, an obnoxious gull wakes me 24
Farewell, thou child of my right hand, and joy 97
Fern Hill [extract] 49
Few things surpass old wine – and they may preach 48
Field Guide 147
The Fired Pot 51
Flight 46–7
A flowery band to bind us to the earth, 123
For the Anniversary of My Death 141
For the first time, now for the first time seen 163
Four Years Later 108–9
Friday Afternoon 38
Friends ask how she copes with his dour silence 89
from your eager mouth / the taste of strawberries 116
The fruit fermented, the sweet flesh would turn sour 120

The Gardener's Daughter [extract] 23
The gentleness of secretaries in the morning is something 27
The ghosts walking, lifting latches 144
A Glimpse 82
A glimpse through an interstice caught 82
Gloire de Dijon 40
go shit / on someone else's head 24
Going Home 125–6
The Good-Morrow 82–3
Grace 170–1
The great bell of the world vibrates and I am drunk 167
Green 163

Had I the heavens' embroidered cloths 96
Hail to thee, blithe Spirit! 150
hands, like X-rays on the glass 22
Happiness 25–6
Haunter of woods, lone wilds and solitudes 154
He altered the expression of my face, / And gave me back my beauty 51
He Wishes for the Cloths of Heaven 96
Helpless among the living and the dead 134
Her lips twitch, try to find the forgotten shape / of my name 104
'Here doth lie / Ben Jonson his best piece of poetry' 97
High Summer 169
His eyes are coals from the middle of Hell 70
Hock and Soda-Water 48
Home is the sailor, home from sea 145
The horizons ring me like faggots 158
The house breathed like a sleeper 143
a house coughed up overnight 66
How Do I Become the Very Ground? 163–4
How do I love thee? Let me count the ways 88
how easily the rain bisects the sky 13
How time turns back and the doubtful season passes 92

I awaken, muddled, to slovenly bedclothes 137
I had not thought that it would be like this 143
'I have answered three questions, and that is enough' 133
I have been here before 127
I have spread my dreams under your feet 97
I have this need for fields 163

I leant upon a coppice gate 20

I love thee freely, as men strive for right 88

I love to see the old heath's withered brake 152

I Loved You 91

I loved you; even now I may confess 91

I met a lady in the meads 94

I must go down to the seas again, to the lonely sea and the sky 139

I never wholly feel that summer is high 169

I only saw him briefly 15

I pray God grant another love you so 93

I set her on my pacing steed 94

I shall but love thee better after death 89

I So Liked Spring 151

I so liked Spring last year 151

I think my love as rare / As any she belied with false compare 86

I used to drop down behind a hedge bush or dyke 153

I wanted to cross the tidal river 26

I was sitting next to the wood burner 18

I wonder, by my troth, what thou and I 82

Ice on the Highway 50

If I when my wife is sleeping 32

If you're to leave this world, you'll leave it here 13

In an imperfect incense 74

In our town, people live in rows 51

In the stillness, everything becomes itself 170

In the worst hour of the worst season 14

In Wales there are jewels 162

In winter I get up at night 64

Inefficient View of a Happy Man 15

Into my lap, a great star will fall . . . 80

it had drunk all the sweetness from the sun 38

it is my spirit that kisses your mouth lightly 84

'It sounds very high' 62

It was not set ticking / by the moving fingers of a craftsman 172

It was the autumn's last day, when the roof 38

It's all there in the disappearing light 125

it's come down with the dusk, left 21

Just off the A5, West of Llangollen 121

Just Once 118

Kisses 87–8

Kisses make men loth to go 87

Kitchen Ghosts 107

La Belle Dame Sans Merci: A Ballad [extract] 94–5

The Last Poem 172–3

The last poem was not wrought 172

Late August, given heavy rain and sun 119

The latest dream I ever dreamt / On the cold hill side 95

A lawn about the shoulders thrown 54

Leaving stains upon the tongue and lust for / Picking 119

Let me but live my life from year to year 135

let me cook for you, a meal so wholesome and blimmin' / pungent 101

Let Nature be your teacher 148

let the storm wash the plates 116

Life 135

The Light Beneath 89–90

Like an unbodied joy whose race is just begun 150

Like the beam of a lightless star 141

The lime a summer home of murmurous wings 23
Live Broadcast 136–7
Living is no laughing matter 33
Look to your lasses, lads, if you can, pull away 112
Love set you going like a fat gold watch 98
Love so alike, that none do slacken, none can die 83
Lowedges 13

The Malvern Hills 124
The Malvern Hills 124
Me and my friends 52
The meadows still as Sunday 168
The moon was a golden petal between 163
Moonlit Apples 117
Morning 27
Morning Song 98–9
Mother's tricks will pass to daughter 64
My face in thine eye, thine in mine appears 83
My heart will keep the courage of the quest 135
My Love bound me with a kiss 87
My mistress' eyes are nothing like the sun 86
My mother is clearing dandelions 105
My mother was an alchemist, she conjured 68
My Mother's Arts 68–9
My Mother's Bathroom Armoury 63–4

Never closer the whole rest of our lives 99
Never did sun more beautifully steep 16
The nineteenth autumn has come upon me 156
Not conscious 171

Not rain but fine mist 106
Now all that is between us is the music 136
Now as I was young and easy under the apple boughs 49
Now her spine is hooked / into a question mark 102
Now the Wolf is in the Cul-de-sac 21–2

O taste and see 53
O Taste and See 53–4
O You Angels, Who Guard the People 143–4
An oddling crow in idle motion swing 152
Of a youth who loves me and whom I love 82
of dancing feet and babies' knees 67
Oh we've got to trust 36
Old Man 128–9
Old Man, or Lad's-love, – in the name there's nothing 128
On Hearing for the First Time 62–3
On Living 33–5
On moon-washed apples of wonder 117
On My First Son 97
Once, in the cool blue middle of a lake 147
One cry, and I stumble from bed, cow-heavy and floral 98
One Day a Student Called me 'Dad' 71–2
Only an avenue, dark, nameless, without end 129
Only Some Spires 160
Only some spires of bright green grass 160
Other little children / Shall bring my boats ashore 140
Our London Underground 73–4

The Pale Horse 104

Perhaps my dogs 122
Please can I have a man 79–80
Please can I have a man who wears
    corduroy 79
*A pleasure worthy of Xerxes, the great
    king* 48
Poem 26–7
**Poem for People That Are
    Understandably too Busy to
    Read Poetry** 58–60

Quarantine 14–15

Rain 134
Rain, midnight rain, nothing but the
    wild rain 134
Reconciliation 80–1
A red apple after dark isn't red 164
Relax. This won't last long 58
Requiem 145
Robins will wear their feathery fire 19
*Rough winds do shake the darling buds
    of May* 90

Sea-Fever 139
The sea is calm tonight 130
Seven buxom women abreast, and
    arm in arm 50
Shall I compare thee to a summer's
    day? 90
She looks up from the potatoes, sees
    him in the garden 89
She's bird-thin 102
*Ships, towers, domes, theatres, and
    temples lie* 16
Silence the village gossip with nutty
    figs 41
Six years now my mother gone to earth
    106
*The sky leans on me, me, the one upright
    / Among the horizontals* 159
A slip of some sort; sleepless or
    Freudian 71

The Small Window 162
The smell of him went soon 110
So let the way wind up the hill or down
    135
*So long lives this, and this gives life to
    thee* 90
Some slow evenings when the light
    hangs late and stubborn in the
    sky 125
Some veil did fall, – I knew it all of yore
    127
Somewhat Unravelled 100–1
Song of Myself [extract] 29–31
Sonnet 18 (Shakespeare) 90–1
Sonnet 43 (Browning) 88–9
Sonnet 130 (Shakespeare) 86
Sonnet XLIII (Millay) 93
The Sound of a Knot Being Untied
    112–13
Spilt 95–6
*the spring which is so full of everything /
    continuing in all directions* 75
Steps echo on terracotta tiles 107–8
Strawberries 115–16
Sudden Light 127
*suddenly, / You're beautiful for as long
    as you live* 60
Summer Holidays 52–3
*summer sang in me / A little while, that
    in me sings no more* 93
Summer with Monika 85–6
Summertime 105
Sundays too my father got up early
    72
Sunrise, the things I offer you 67
The sweeping up the heart 109
A sweet disorder in the dress 54
Sweet is the lore which Nature brings
    149

The Tables Turned 148–9
ten milk bottles standing in the hall
    85

Then I will no longer / Find myself in life as in a strange garment 141
Theory of Light 164–5
There are no gods 28–9
There are no gods, and you can please yourself 28
There is no life higher than the grasstops 158
There were never strawberries 115
There will come soft rains 19
There will come soft rains and the smell of the ground 19
There's just no accounting for happiness 25
They are waiting for me somewhere beyond Eden Rock 142
They dream of the acorned swill of the world 168
They must perforce trudge thus, to keep upright 50
A thing of beauty is a joy for ever 123
Thirteen Ways with Figs 41–5
This dew, light as footsteps of the dead 106
This earth will grow cold one day 35
This house has been far out at sea all night 76
This part of the river expects to be seen, for it has drawn you there 155
This star is only an augury of the morning 166
Those Winter Sundays 72
Thou art unseen, but yet I hear thy shrill delight 151
A thousand webs barely contain the green thrum 167
Tides 65–6
till we both of us / are more glorious / and more sunny 37
The tiny petals of the mountain-ash 131
To a Skylark [extract] 150–1
to be shaken off with the weight of childhood 95

To swing the gate shut and latch it 121
To the Fox Fern 154
Today's Headlines 18
The Tom-Cat 69–70
Too late to go out and nowhere to go 136
A touch of cold in the Autumn night 166
Transparently in sunshine quivering 160
Tread softly because you tread on my dreams 97
The trees are in their autumn beauty 156
Trust 36–7
Try to praise the mutilated world 12
Try to praise the mutilated world 12
The Twist in the River 155–6
Tŷ Unnos (One Night House) 67–8

Under Milk Wood [extract] 168
Under the Lemon Tree 106–7
Under the wide and starry sky 145
until the final light-show of applause 137
Up! up! my Friend, and quit your books 148
An upper chamber in a darkened house 131
An upper chamber in a darkened house 131

a vast geometry of pines 21
Vie with that draught of hock and soda-water 48

waiting / a quiet unscowling moment longer / for him to return 76
Waiting for the Bus 122
Washing My Mother's Hair 102–3
The washing never gets done 66
The washing never gets done 66–7
We breathe into sleep, the low

rumble of rain on the roof 46
we must live as if we will never die 35
We shall never forget nor escape you 110
The wealth is for the few / And chosen 162
Well, I am thinking this may be my last 84
What are deep? The ocean and truth 137
What are Heavy? 137
What are heavy? Sea-sand and sorrow 137
what did I know / of love's austere and lonely offices? 68
What lips my lips have kissed, and where, and why 93
When all the others were away at Mass 99
When all the others were away at Mass 99
When she rises in the morning 40
When the bare feet of the baby beat across the grass 61
When the sky pops and hisses with stars 45
Where Go the Boats? 140
Where the humming-bird shimmers, where the neck of . . . 30
Where the sea meets the moon-blanched land 130
Where winter wolves bark amid wastes of snow and icicled trees 30
Whistle and I will hear / and come again another evening 84
who makes me creamy curries from fresh lemongrass 79
Who shall say I am not / the happy genius of my household? 32
The Wild Swans at Coole 156–7
Wind 76–7
A wind has brought the musk of thirty fields 166

Winds stampeding the fields under the window 73
The windy clanging of the minster clock 23
Wine Glasses 57
Wine glasses must be washed first 57
wingless car and frost bitten strawberries 124
the wistful stars / With white faces like town children 167
With her little bare feet in my hands 61
with nothing to offer the people you love / but damp fingers 96
With the swing of his demon's tail 70–1
Woman's flesh a fading treasure 64
The Word 137–8
Work without Hope 17
The world is / not with us enough 53
Wrap around the weeping skin in a muslin cloth 42
Wuthering Heights 158–60

Yet loud their laughter as they stagger and slide! 50
Yet you balanced an eel on the end of your nose 133
You are old, Father William 132–3
'You are old, Father William,' the young man said 132
You ate that first one and its flesh was sweet 119
You took handfuls of sea 95
You'll be greeted 46
Young salt-footed fools, you know there are no ends 165
your bald cry / Took its place among the elements 98
your soul was assaulted / by Satan's fresh espresso smell? 46
You've been living for this for weeks 170
You've seen the refugees going nowhere 12